MznLnx

Missing Links Exam Preps

Exam Prep for

Vector Calculus

Marsden & Tromba, 5th Edition

The MznLnx Exam Prep is your link from the texbook and lecture to your exams.
The MznLnx Exam Preps are unauthorized and comprehensive reviews of your textbooks.

All material provided by MznLnx and Rico Publications (c) 2010
Textbook publishers and textbook authors do not particpate in or contribute to these reviews.

MznLnx

Rico
Publications

Exam Prep for Vector Calculus
5th Edition
Marsden & Tromba

Publisher: Raymond Houge
Assistant Editor: Michael Rouger
Text and Cover Designer: Lisa Buckner
Marketing Manager: Sara Swagger
Project Manager, Editorial Production: Jerry Emerson
Art Director: Vernon Lowerui

Product Manager: Dave Mason
Editorial Assitant: Rachel Guzmanji
Pedagogy: Debra Long
Cover Image: Jim Reed/Getty Images
Text and Cover Printer: City Printing, Inc.
Compositor: Media Mix, Inc.

(c) 2010 Rico Publications
ALL RIGHTS RESERVED. No part of this work covered by the copyright may be reproduced or used in any form or by an means--graphic, electronic, or mechanical, including photocopying, recording, taping, Web distribution, information storage, and retrieval systems, or in any other manner--without the written permission of the publisher.

For more information about our products, contact us at:
Dave.Mason@RicoPublications.com

For permission to use material from this text or product, submit a request online to:
Dave.Mason@RicoPublications.com

Printed in the United States
ISBN:

Contents

CHAPTER 1
The Geometry of Euclidean Space — 1

CHAPTER 2
Differentiation — 24

CHAPTER 3
Higher-Order Derivatives; Maxima and Minima — 40

CHAPTER 4
Vector-Valued Functions — 59

CHAPTER 5
Double and Triple Integrals — 78

CHAPTER 6
The Change of Variables Formula and Applications of Integration — 88

CHAPTER 7
Integrals Over Paths and Surfaces — 102

CHAPTER 8
The Integral Theorems of Vector Analysis — 122

ANSWER KEY — 139

TO THE STUDENT

COMPREHENSIVE

The *MznLnx* Exam Prep series is designed to help you pass your exams. Editors at MznLnx review your textbooks and then prepare these practice exams to help you master the textbook material. Unlike study guides, workbooks, and practice tests provided by the texbook publisher and textbook authors, *MznLnx* gives you **all** of the material in each chapter in exam form, not just samples, so you can be sure to nail your exam.

MECHANICAL

The MznLnx Exam Prep series creates exams that will help you learn the subject matter as well as test you on your understanding. Each question is designed to help you master the concept. Just working through the exams, you gain an understanding of the subject--its a simple mechanical process that produces success.

INTEGRATED STUDY GUIDE AND REVIEW

MznLnx is not just a set of exams designed to test you, its also a comprehensive review of the subject content. Each exam question is also a review of the concept, making sure that you will get the answer correct without having to go to other sources of material. You learn as you go! Its the easiest way to pass an exam.

HUMOR

Studying can be tedious and dry. MznLnx's instructional design includes moderate humor within the exam questions on occassion, to break the tedium and revitalize the brain

Chapter 1. The Geometry of Euclidean Space

1. In mathematics, _____ are a non-commutative extension of complex numbers. They were first described by the Irish mathematician Sir William Rowan Hamilton in 1843 and applied to mechanics in three-dimensional space. At first, _____ were regarded as pathological, because they disobeyed the commutative law ab = ba. Although they have been superseded in most applications by vectors, they still find uses in both theoretical and applied mathematics, in particular for calculations involving three-dimensional rotations, such as in 3D computer graphics.
   a. Quaternions0
   b. Thing
   c. Undefined
   d. Undefined

2. _____ is a set, with some particular properties and usually some additional structure, such as the operations of addition or multiplication, for instance.
   a. Thing
   b. Space0
   c. Undefined
   d. Undefined

3. Around 300 BC, the Greek mathematician Euclid laid down the rules of what has now come to be called "Euclidean geometry", which is the study of the relationships between angles and distances in space. Euclid first developed "plane geometry" which dealt with the geometry of two-dimensional objects on a flat surface. He then went on to develop "solid geometry" which analyzed the geometry of three-dimensional objects. All of the axioms of Euclid have been encoded into an abstract mathematical space known as a two- or three-dimensional _____. These mathematical spaces may be extended to apply to any dimension, and such a space is called an n-dimensional _____.
   a. Thing
   b. Euclidean space0
   c. Undefined
   d. Undefined

4. In physics and in _____ calculus, a spatial _____, or simply _____, is a concept characterized by a magnitude and a direction.
   a. Thing
   b. Vector0
   c. Undefined
   d. Undefined

5. In mathematics, a _____ is an n-tuple with n being 3.
   a. Thing
   b. Triple0
   c. Undefined
   d. Undefined

6. In mathematics, a _____ may be described informally as a number that can be given by an infinite decimal representation.
   a. Thing
   b. Real number0
   c. Undefined
   d. Undefined

7. In geometry, two lines or planes if one falls on the other in such a way as to create congruent adjacent angles. The term may be used as a noun or adjective. Thus, referring to Figure 1, the line AB is the _____ to CD through the point B.
   a. Thing
   b. Perpendicular0
   c. Undefined
   d. Undefined

8. A _____ is a set of numbers that designate location in a given reference system, such as x,y in a planar _____ system or an x,y,z in a three-dimensional _____ system.
   a. Coordinate0
   b. Thing
   c. Undefined
   d. Undefined

Chapter 1. The Geometry of Euclidean Space

9. In mathematics, _____ is an elementary arithmetic operation. When one of the numbers is a whole number, _____ is the repeated sum of the other number.
   a. Multiplication0
   b. Thing
   c. Undefined
   d. Undefined

10. In linear algebra, real numbers are called scalars and relate to vectors in a vector space through the operation of _____ multiplication, in which a vector can be multiplied by a number to produce another vector.
    a. Thing
    b. Scalar0
    c. Undefined
    d. Undefined

11. _____ is one of the basic operations defining a vector space in linear algebra.
    a. Thing
    b. Scalar multiplication0
    c. Undefined
    d. Undefined

12. An _____ is a collection of two not necessarily distinct objects, one of which is distinguished as the first coordinate and the other as the second coordinate.
    a. Thing
    b. Ordered pair0
    c. Undefined
    d. Undefined

13. In mathematics, the conjugate _____ or adjoint matrix of an m-by-n matrix A with complex entries is the n-by-m matrix A* obtained from A by taking the transpose and then taking the complex conjugate of each entry.
    a. Thing
    b. Pairs0
    c. Undefined
    d. Undefined

14. _____ is a branch of mathematics concerning the study of structure, relation and quantity.
    a. Algebra0
    b. Concept
    c. Undefined
    d. Undefined

15. In mathematics, in the field of group theory, a _____ of a group is a quasisimple subnormal subgroup.
    a. Component0
    b. Concept
    c. Undefined
    d. Undefined

16. The _____ of a mathematical object is its size: a property by which it can be larger or smaller than other objects of the same kind; in technical terms, an ordering of the class of objects to which it belongs.
    a. Magnitude0
    b. Thing
    c. Undefined
    d. Undefined

17. The _____, the average in everyday English, which is also called the arithmetic _____ (and is distinguished from the geometric _____ or harmonic _____). The average is also called the sample _____. The expected value of a random variable, which is also called the population _____.
    a. Mean0
    b. Thing
    c. Undefined
    d. Undefined

18. A _____ is a four-sided plane figure that has two sets of opposite parallel sides.

Chapter 1. The Geometry of Euclidean Space

a. Parallelogram0
c. Undefined
b. Concept
d. Undefined

19. In mathematics, a _____ is a two-dimensional manifold or surface that is perfectly flat.
a. Thing
c. Undefined
b. Plane0
d. Undefined

20. In geometry, _____ angles are angles that have a common ray coming out of the vertex going between two other rays.
a. Adjacent0
c. Undefined
b. Concept
d. Undefined

21. In geometry, a line _____ is a part of a line that is bounded by two end points, and contains every point on the line between its end points.
a. Segment0
c. Undefined
b. Concept
d. Undefined

22. A _____ is the result of the addition of a set of numbers. The numbers may be natural numbers, complex numbers, matrices, or still more complicated objects. An infinite _____ is a subtle procedure known as a series.
a. Sum0
c. Undefined
b. Thing
d. Undefined

23. A _____ is a part of a line that is bounded by two end points, and contains every point on the line between its end points.
a. Line segment0
c. Undefined
b. Thing
d. Undefined

24. A _____ can refer to a line joining two nonadjacent vertices of a polygon or polyhedron, or in some contexts any upward or downward sloping line. .
a. Diagonal0
c. Undefined
b. Thing
d. Undefined

25. In mathematics, a _____ is a demonstration that, assuming certain axioms, some statement is necessarily true.
a. Thing
c. Undefined
b. Proof0
d. Undefined

26. In geometry, an _____ is a point at which a line segment or ray terminates.
a. Thing
c. Undefined
b. Endpoint0
d. Undefined

27. A _____ is one of the basic shapes of geometry: a polygon with three vertices and three sides which are straight line segments.
a. Thing
c. Undefined
b. Triangle0
d. Undefined

28. Three or more points that lie on the same line are called _____ .

a. Thing
b. Collinear0
c. Undefined
d. Undefined

29. A _____ ratio, also called, Lift-to-drag ratio, _____ number, or finesse, is an aviation term that refers to the distance an aircraft will move forward for any given amount of lost altitude .
a. Thing
b. Glide0
c. Undefined
d. Undefined

30. The _____ rule, also known as a slipstick, is a mechanical analog computer, consisting of at least two finely divided scales , most often a fixed outer pair and a movable inner one, with a sliding window called the cursor.
a. Thing
b. Slide0
c. Undefined
d. Undefined

31. In mathematics, the _____ of a coordinate system is the point where the axes of the system intersect.
a. Origin0
b. Thing
c. Undefined
d. Undefined

32. In Euclidean geometry, a _____ is moving every point a constant distance in a specified direction.
a. Translation0
b. Concept
c. Undefined
d. Undefined

33. A _____ is a movement of an object in a circular motion. A two-dimensional object rotates around a center (or point) of _____. A three-dimensional object rotates around a line called an axis. If the axis of _____ is within the body, the body is said to rotate upon itself, or spin—which implies relative speed and perhaps free-movement with angular momentum. A circular motion about an external point, e.g. the Earth about the Sun, is called an orbit or more properly an orbital revolution.
a. Thing
b. Rotation0
c. Undefined
d. Undefined

34. In mathematics, a _____ is any one of several different types of functions, mappings, operations, or transformations.
a. Projection0
b. Thing
c. Undefined
d. Undefined

35. An _____ is when two lines intersect somewhere on a plane creating a right angle at intersection
a. Thing
b. Axes0
c. Undefined
d. Undefined

36. A _____ of a number is the product of that number with any integer.
a. Thing
b. Multiple0
c. Undefined
d. Undefined

37. In mathematics, science including computer science, linguistics and engineering, an _____ is, generally speaking, an independent variable or input to a function.

a. Thing
b. Argument0
c. Undefined
d. Undefined

38. In mathematics, the additive inverse, or _____ of a number n is the number that, when added to n, yields zero. The additive inverse of n is denoted −n. For example, 7 is −7, because 7 + (−7) = 0, and the additive inverse of −0.3 is 0.3, because −0.3 + 0.3 = 0.
    a. Thing
    b. Opposite0
    c. Undefined
    d. Undefined

39. In mathematics, the _____ of a number n is the number that, when added to n, yields zero. The _____ of n is denoted −n. For example, 7 is −7, because 7 + (−7) = 0, and the _____ of −0.3 is 0.3, because −0.3 + 0.3 = 0.
    a. Additive inverse0
    b. Thing
    c. Undefined
    d. Undefined

40. _____ also called natural basis or canonical basis of the n-dimensional Euclidean space Rn is the basis obtained by taking the n basis vectors
    a. Standard basis0
    b. Thing
    c. Undefined
    d. Undefined

41. In mathematics, a _____ is a statement that can be proved on the basis of explicitly stated or previously agreed assumptions.
    a. Theorem0
    b. Thing
    c. Undefined
    d. Undefined

42. _____ is the middle point of a line segment.
    a. Thing
    b. Midpoint0
    c. Undefined
    d. Undefined

43. In mathematics, _____ are two-dimensional manifolds or surfaces that are perfectly flat.
    a. Planes0
    b. Thing
    c. Undefined
    d. Undefined

44. A _____ is the quantity that defines certain relatively constant characteristics of systems or functions..
    a. Thing
    b. Parameter0
    c. Undefined
    d. Undefined

45. In mathematics, a _____ is a constant multiplicative factor of a certain object. The object can be such things as a variable, a vector, a function, etc. For example, the _____ of $9x^2$ is 9.
    a. Thing
    b. Coefficient0
    c. Undefined
    d. Undefined

46. _____ statistics are statistics that estimate population parameters.
    a. Thing
    b. Parametric0
    c. Undefined
    d. Undefined

Chapter 1. The Geometry of Euclidean Space

47. In linear algebra and related areas of mathematics, the null vector or _____ is the vector in Euclidean space, all of whose components are zero.
   a. Thing
   b. Zero vector0
   c. Undefined
   d. Undefined

48. In mathematics, _____ bear slight similarity to functions: they allow one to use arbitrary values, called parameters, in place of independent variables in equations, which in turn provide values for dependent variables. A simple kinematical example is when one uses a time parameter to determine the position, velocity, and other information about a body in motion.
   a. Parametric equations0
   b. Thing
   c. Undefined
   d. Undefined

49. In mathematics, an _____ is a statement about the relative size or order of two objects.
   a. Inequality0
   b. Thing
   c. Undefined
   d. Undefined

50. Deductive _____ is the kind of _____ in which the conclusion is necessitated by, or reached from, previously known facts (the premises).
   a. Thing
   b. Reasoning0
   c. Undefined
   d. Undefined

51. In mathematics, a _____ case is a limiting case in which a class of object changes its nature so as to belong to another, usually simpler, class.
   a. Thing
   b. Degenerate0
   c. Undefined
   d. Undefined

52. In mathematics and its applications, a _____ is a system for assigning an n-tuple of numbers or scalars to each point in an n-dimensional space.
   a. Concept
   b. Coordinate system0
   c. Undefined
   d. Undefined

53. Mathematical _____ is used to represent ideas.
   a. Notation0
   b. Thing
   c. Undefined
   d. Undefined

54. Compass and straightedge or ruler-and-compass _____ is the _____ of lengths or angles using only an idealized ruler and compass.
   a. Thing
   b. Construction0
   c. Undefined
   d. Undefined

55. In mathematics, the _____ of two sets A and B is the set that contains all elements of A that also belong to B (or equivalently, all elements of B that also belong to A), but no other elements.
   a. Intersection0
   b. Thing
   c. Undefined
   d. Undefined

56. In geometry, a _____ is a three-dimensional figure formed by six parallelograms.

a. Thing
b. Parallelepiped0
c. Undefined
d. Undefined

57. In mathematics, a _____ is the result of multiplying, or an expression that identifies factors to be multiplied.
a. Product0
b. Thing
c. Undefined
d. Undefined

58. In common philosophical language, a proposition or _____, is the content of an assertion, that is, it is true-or-false and defined by the meaning of a particular piece of language.
a. Statement0
b. Concept
c. Undefined
d. Undefined

59. A _____ is a quantity that denotes the proportional amount or magnitude of one quantity relative to another.
a. Thing
b. Ratio0
c. Undefined
d. Undefined

60. In probability theory and statistics, a _____ is a number dividing the higher half of a sample, a population, or a probability distribution from the lower half.
a. Median0
b. Concept
c. Undefined
d. Undefined

61. A _____ is a simplified and structured visual representation of concepts, ideas, constructions, relations, statistical data, anatomy etc used in all aspects of human activities to visualize and clarify the topic.
a. Diagram0
b. Thing
c. Undefined
d. Undefined

62. Mathematical _____ are demonstrations that, assuming certain axioms, some statement is necessarily true.
a. Proofs0
b. Thing
c. Undefined
d. Undefined

63. _____ is a relation in Euclidean geometry among the three sides of a right triangle.
a. Thing
b. Pythagorean Theorem0
c. Undefined
d. Undefined

64. _____ in a normed vector space is a vector whose length, or magnitude is 1.
a. Thing
b. Unit vector0
c. Undefined
d. Undefined

65. In geometry, an _____ polygon is a polygon which has all sides of the same length.
a. Thing
b. Equilateral0
c. Undefined
d. Undefined

66. _____ is a trigonemtric function that is important when studying triangles and modeling periodic phenomena, among other applications.

Chapter 1. The Geometry of Euclidean Space

   a. Sine0
   c. Undefined

   b. Thing
   d. Undefined

67. An _____ is a straight line around which a geometric figure can be rotated.
   a. Axis0
   c. Undefined

   b. Thing
   d. Undefined

68. A _____ is a mathematical statement which follows easily from a previously proven statement, typically a mathematical theorem.
   a. Corollary0
   c. Undefined

   b. Thing
   d. Undefined

69. Two mathematical objects are equal if and only if they are precisely the same in every way. This defines a binary relation, _____, denoted by the sign of _____ "=" in such a way that the statement "x = y" means that x and y are equal.
   a. Thing
   c. Undefined

   b. Equality0
   d. Undefined

70. In mathematics, the _____, also known as the scalar product, is a binary operation which takes two vectors over the real numbers R and returns a real-valued scalar quantity. It is the standard inner product of the Euclidean space.
   a. Dot product0
   c. Undefined

   b. Thing
   d. Undefined

71. In mathematics, _____ is synonymous with perpendicular when used as a simple adjective that is not part of any longer phrase with a standard definition. It means at right angles. It comes from the Greek á½€Ï Î¸ÏŒÏ, orthos, meaning "straight", used by Euclid to mean right; and Î³Ï‰Î½Î¯Î± gonia, meaning angle. Two streets that cross each other at a right angle are _____ to one another.
   a. Orthogonal0
   c. Undefined

   b. Thing
   d. Undefined

72. In linear algebra, two vectors in an inner product space are _____ if they are orthogonal (their inner product is 0) and both of unit length (the norm of each is 1). A set of vectors which is pairwise _____ (any two vectors in it are _____) is called an _____ set. A basis which forms an _____ set is called an _____ basis.
   a. Thing
   c. Undefined

   b. Orthonormal0
   d. Undefined

73. _____ is the theorem stating that for any triangle, the measure of a given side must be less than the sum of the other two sides but greater than the difference between the two sides.
   a. Thing
   c. Undefined

   b. Triangle inequality0
   d. Undefined

74. In mathematics, an inequality is a statement about the relative size or order of two objects. For example 14 > 10, or 14 is _____ 10.
   a. Greater than0
   c. Undefined

   b. Thing
   d. Undefined

75. _____ is the transport of people on a trip/journey or the process or time involved in a person or object moving from one location to another.
   a. Travel0
   b. Thing
   c. Undefined
   d. Undefined

76. A _____ is a unit of length in the metric system, equal to one thousand metres, the current SI base unit of length
   a. Kilometer0
   b. Thing
   c. Undefined
   d. Undefined

77. _____ of an object is its speed in a particular direction.
   a. Velocity0
   b. Thing
   c. Undefined
   d. Undefined

78. A _____ is a special kind of ratio, indicating a relationship between two measurements with different units, such as miles to gallons or cents to pounds.
   a. Thing
   b. Rate0
   c. Undefined
   d. Undefined

79. The _____ of measurement are a globally standardized and modernized form of the metric system.
   a. Units0
   b. Thing
   c. Undefined
   d. Undefined

80. In mathematics and the mathematical sciences, a _____ is a fixed, but possibly unspecified, value. This is in contrast to a variable, which is not fixed.
   a. Constant0
   b. Thing
   c. Undefined
   d. Undefined

81. In geometry, an _____ of a triangle is a straight line through a vertex and perpendicular to (i.e. forming a right angle with) the opposite side or an extension of the opposite side.
   a. Altitude0
   b. Concept
   c. Undefined
   d. Undefined

82. In physics, _____ is an influence that may cause an object to accelerate. It may be experienced as a lift, a push, or a pull. The actual acceleration of the body is determined by the vector sum of all forces acting on it, known as net _____ or resultant _____.
   a. Force0
   b. Thing
   c. Undefined
   d. Undefined

83. In mathematics, the _____ is two monic polynomials P and Q over a field k.
   a. Resultant0
   b. Thing
   c. Undefined
   d. Undefined

84. _____ is a vector produced when two or more forces act upon a single object.
   a. Thing
   b. Resultant force0
   c. Undefined
   d. Undefined

Chapter 1. The Geometry of Euclidean Space

85. A _____, sea mile or nautimile is a unit of length. It is accepted for use with the International System of Units (SI), but it is not an SI unit.[1] The _____ is used around the world for maritime and aviation purposes. It is commonly used in international law and treaties, especially regarding the limits of territorial waters. It developed from the geographical mile.
   a. Nautical mile0
   b. Thing
   c. Undefined
   d. Undefined

86. A _____ is a method for fastening or securing linear material such as rope by tying or interweaving. It may consist of a length of one or more segments of rope, string, webbing, twine, strap or even chain interwoven so as to create in the line the ability to bind to itself or to some other object - the "load". Knots have been the subject of interest both for their ancient origins, common use, and the mathematical implications of _____ theory.
   a. Knot0
   b. Thing
   c. Undefined
   d. Undefined

87. A _____ is a unit of length, usually used to measure distance, in a number of different systems, including Imperial units, United States customary units and Norwegian/Swedish mil. Its size can vary from system to system, but in each is between 1 and 10 kilometers. In contemporary English contexts _____ refers to either:
   a. Mile0
   b. Thing
   c. Undefined
   d. Undefined

88. _____ is a unit of speed, expressing the number of international miles covered per hour.
   a. Miles per hour0
   b. Thing
   c. Undefined
   d. Undefined

89. In astronomy, geography, geometry and related sciences and contexts, a plane is said to be _____ at a given point if it is locally perpendicular to the gradient of the gravity field, i.e., with the direction of the gravitational force at that point.
   a. Thing
   b. Horizontal0
   c. Undefined
   d. Undefined

90. In Euclidean geometry, a uniform _____ is a linear transformation that enlargers or diminishes objects, and whose _____ factor is the same in all directions. This is also called homothethy.
   a. Thing
   b. Scale0
   c. Undefined
   d. Undefined

91. _____ is a branch of mathematics which deals with triangles, particularly triangles in a plane where one angle of the triangle is 90 degrees, and a variety of other topological relations such as spheres, in other branches, such as spherical _____.
   a. Thing
   b. Trigonometry0
   c. Undefined
   d. Undefined

92. Sir Isaac _____, was an English physicist, mathematician, astronomer, natural philosopher, and alchemist, regarded by many as the greatest figure in the history of science
   a. Person
   b. Newton0
   c. Undefined
   d. Undefined

Chapter 1. The Geometry of Euclidean Space

93. The _____ is a unit of plane angle. It is represented by the symbol "rad" or, more rarely, by the superscript c (for "circular measure"). For example, an angle of 1.2 radians would be written "1.2 rad" or "1.2c" (second symbol can produce confusion with centigrads).
   a. Thing
   b. Radian0
   c. Undefined
   d. Undefined

94. _____ is a binary operation on two vectors in a three-dimensional Euclidean space that results in another vector which is perpedicular to the two input vectors.
   a. Cross product0
   b. Thing
   c. Undefined
   d. Undefined

95. In mathematics, a _____ is a rectangular table of numbers or, more generally, a table consisting of abstract quantities that can be added and multiplied.
   a. Thing
   b. Matrix0
   c. Undefined
   d. Undefined

96. In algebra, a _____ is a function depending on n that associates a scalar, det(A), to every n×n square matrix A.
   a. Thing
   b. Determinant0
   c. Undefined
   d. Undefined

97. In logic and mathematics, logical _____ is a logical relation that holds between a set T of formulas and a formula B when every model (or interpretation or valuation) of T is also a model of B.
   a. Implication0
   b. Concept
   c. Undefined
   d. Undefined

98. In computer science an _____ is a data structure that consists of a group of elements having a single name that are accessed by indexing. In most programming languages each element has the same data type and the _____ occupies a continuous area of storage.
   a. Thing
   b. Array0
   c. Undefined
   d. Undefined

99. In mathematics, a matrix can be thought of as each row or _____ being a vector. Hence, a space formed by row vectors or _____ vectors are said to be a row space or a _____ space.
   a. Column0
   b. Concept
   c. Undefined
   d. Undefined

100. The plus and _____ signs are mathematical symbols used to represent the notions of positive and negative as well as the operations of addition and subtraction.
   a. Thing
   b. Minus0
   c. Undefined
   d. Undefined

101. Colin _____ was a Scottish mathematician.
   a. Maclaurin0
   b. Person
   c. Undefined
   d. Undefined

Chapter 1. The Geometry of Euclidean Space

102. In mathematics, the word _____ is used informally to refer to certain distinct bodies of knowledge about mathematics.
   a. Theoretical0
   b. Thing
   c. Undefined
   d. Undefined

103. Alexandre-Théophile _____ was a French musician and chemist who worked with Bezout and Lavoisier; his name is now principally associated with determinant theory in mathematics. He was born in Paris, and died there.
   a. Vandermonde0
   b. Person
   c. Undefined
   d. Undefined

104. In plane geometry, a _____ is a polygon with four equal sides, four right angles, and parallel opposite sides. In algebra, the _____ of a number is that number multiplied by itself.
   a. Square0
   b. Thing
   c. Undefined
   d. Undefined

105. In mathematics, a _____ of a number x is a number r such that $r^2 = x$, or in words, a number r whose square (the result of multiplying the number by itself) is x.
   a. Square root0
   b. Thing
   c. Undefined
   d. Undefined

106. In mathematics, a _____ of a complex-valued function f is a member x of the domain of f such that f(x) vanishes at x, that is, x : f (x) = 0.
   a. Thing
   b. Root0
   c. Undefined
   d. Undefined

107. _____ the expected value of a random variable displays the average or central value of the variable. It is a summary value of the distribution of the variable.
   a. Determining0
   b. Thing
   c. Undefined
   d. Undefined

108. An _____ is a combination of numbers, operators, grouping symbols and/or free variables and bound variables arranged in a meaningful way which can be evaluated..
   a. Thing
   b. Expression0
   c. Undefined
   d. Undefined

109. An _____ is an equality that remains true regardless of the values of any variables that appear within it, to distinguish it from an equality which is true under more particular conditions.
   a. Thing
   b. Identity0
   c. Undefined
   d. Undefined

110. In mathematics, the _____ (or modulus) of a real number is its numerical value without regard to its sign.
   a. Absolute value0
   b. Thing
   c. Undefined
   d. Undefined

Chapter 1. The Geometry of Euclidean Space

111. In geometry, a _____ is a special kind of point, usually a corner of a polygon, polyhedron, or higher dimensional polytope. In the geometry of curves a _____ is a point of where the first derivative of curvature is zero. In graph theory, a _____ is the fundamental unit out of which graphs are formed
   a. Vertex0
   b. Thing
   c. Undefined
   d. Undefined

112. The _____ of a solid object is the three-dimensional concept of how much space it occupies, often quantified numerically.
   a. Thing
   b. Volume0
   c. Undefined
   d. Undefined

113. One of the three formats applicable to a quadratic function is the _____ which is defined as $f = ax^2 + bx + c$.
   a. General form0
   b. Thing
   c. Undefined
   d. Undefined

114. In mathematics, a _____ is a polynomial equation of the third degree.
   a. Cubic equation0
   b. Thing
   c. Undefined
   d. Undefined

115. _____ is the name for any one of many units of measure used by various ancient peoples and is among the first recorded units of length.
   a. Cubit0
   b. Thing
   c. Undefined
   d. Undefined

116. _____ or Girolamo Cardano was a celebrated Italian Renaissance mathematician, physician, astrologer, and gambler.
   a. Gerolamo Cardano0
   b. Person
   c. Undefined
   d. Undefined

117. In mathematics, a _____ or rhodonea curve is a sinusoid plotted in polar coordinates.
   a. Rose0
   b. Thing
   c. Undefined
   d. Undefined

118. _____ was a German mathematician and philosopher. He invented calculus independently of Newton, and his notation is the one in general use since.
   a. Person
   b. Leibniz0
   c. Undefined
   d. Undefined

119. _____ is a mathematical subject that includes the study of limits, derivatives, integrals, and power series and constitutes a major part of modern university curriculum.
   a. Thing
   b. Calculus0
   c. Undefined
   d. Undefined

120. A _____ is a number that is less than zero.

a. Negative number0
b. Thing
c. Undefined
d. Undefined

121. In mathematics, an _____ number is a complex number whose square is a negative real number. They were defined in 1572 by Rafael Bombelli.
   a. Thing
   b. Imaginary0
   c. Undefined
   d. Undefined

122. In geometry, the relations of _____ are those such as 'lies on' between points and lines (as in 'point P lies on line L'), and 'intersects' (as in 'line L_1 intersects line L_2', in three-dimensional space). That is, they are the binary relations describing how subsets meet.
   a. Thing
   b. Incidence0
   c. Undefined
   d. Undefined

123. In mathematics, a _____ is a number in the form of a + bi where a and b are real numbers, and i is the imaginary unit, with the property i 2 = −1. The real number a is called the real part of the _____, and the real number b is the imaginary part.
   a. Thing
   b. Complex number0
   c. Undefined
   d. Undefined

124. _____ algebra (sometimes called General algebra) is the field of mathematics that studies the ideas common to all algebraic structures.
   a. Thing
   b. Universal0
   c. Undefined
   d. Undefined

125. Leonhard _____ was a pioneering Swiss mathematician and physicist, who spent most of his life in Russia and Germany.
   a. Person
   b. Euler0
   c. Undefined
   d. Undefined

126. _____ was a pioneering Swiss mathematician and physicist, who spent most of his life in Russia and Germany.
   a. Leonhard Euler0
   b. Person
   c. Undefined
   d. Undefined

127. _____ has many meanings, most of which simply .
   a. Thing
   b. Power0
   c. Undefined
   d. Undefined

128. A _____ is a symbolic representation denoting a quantity or expression. It often represents an "unknown" quantity that has the potential to change.
   a. Thing
   b. Variable0
   c. Undefined
   d. Undefined

129. _____ was a German mathematician and scientist of profound genius who contributed significantly to many fields, including number theory, analysis, differential geometry, geodesy, magnetism, astronomy, and optics.

a. Karl Friedrich Gauss0   b. Person
c. Undefined   d. Undefined

130. In mathematics, a _____ is an expression that is constructed from one or more variables and constants, using only the operations of addition, subtraction, multiplication, and constant positive whole number exponents. is a _____. Note in particular that division by an expression containing a variable is not in general allowed in polynomials. [1]
  a. Thing   b. Polynomial0
  c. Undefined   d. Undefined

131. A _____ is traditionally an infinitesimally small change in a variable.
  a. Differential0   b. Thing
  c. Undefined   d. Undefined

132. _____, a field in mathematics, is the study of how functions change when their inputs change. The primary object of study in _____ is the derivative.
  a. Thing   b. Differential calculus0
  c. Undefined   d. Undefined

133. The mathematical concept of a _____ expresses the intuitive idea of deterministic dependence between two quantities, one of which is viewed as primary and the other as secondary. A _____ then is a way to associate a unique output for each input of a specified type, for example, a real number or an element of a given set.
  a. Thing   b. Function0
  c. Undefined   d. Undefined

134. In number theory, the _____ of arithmetic (or unique factorization theorem) states that every natural number greater than 1 can be written as a unique product of prime numbers.
  a. Concept   b. Fundamental theorem0
  c. Undefined   d. Undefined

135. _____ states that every non-zero single-variable polynomial, with complex coefficients, has exactly as many complex roots as its degree, if repeated roots are counted up to their multiplicity.
  a. Fundamental theorem of algebra0   b. Thing
  c. Undefined   d. Undefined

136. Sir _____ was an Irish mathematician, physicist, and astronomer who made important contributions to the development of optics, dynamics, and algebra. His discovery of quaternions is perhaps his best known investigation.
  a. Person   b. William Rowan Hamilton0
  c. Undefined   d. Undefined

137. _____ is the scientific study of celestial objects such as stars, planets, comets, and galaxies; and phenomena that originate outside the Earth's atmosphere.
  a. Astronomy0   b. Thing
  c. Undefined   d. Undefined

138. _____ means of or relating to the French philosopher and mathematician RenÃ© Descartes.

16 **Chapter 1. The Geometry of Euclidean Space**

    a. Thing   b. Cartesian0
    c. Undefined   d. Undefined

139. _____ Any process by which a specified characteristic usually amplitude of the output of a device is prevented from exceeding a predetermined value.
    a. Limiting0   b. Thing
    c. Undefined   d. Undefined

140. _____, Greek for "knowledge of nature," is the branch of science concerned with the discovery and characterization of universal laws which govern matter, energy, space, and time.
    a. Physics0   b. Thing
    c. Undefined   d. Undefined

141. _____ is a property that a binary operation can have.
    a. Thing   b. Associative law0
    c. Undefined   d. Undefined

142. In probability theory, _____ are various sets of outcomes (a subset of the sample space) to which a probability is assigned.
    a. Events0   b. Thing
    c. Undefined   d. Undefined

143. _____ are objects, characters, or other concrete representations of ideas, concepts, or other abstractions.
    a. Symbols0   b. Thing
    c. Undefined   d. Undefined

144. In mathematics, a _____ is a countable collection of open covers of a topological space that satisfies certain separation axioms.
    a. Development0   b. Thing
    c. Undefined   d. Undefined

145. _____ is dedicated to the interests of mathematical research and scholarship, which it does with various publications and conferences as well as annual monetary awards to mathematicians.
    a. American Mathematical Society0   b. Thing
    c. Undefined   d. Undefined

146. _____ is the fee paid on borrowed money.
    a. Interest0   b. Thing
    c. Undefined   d. Undefined

147. There are two main approaches to _____ in mathematics. They are the model theory of _____ and the proof theory of _____.
    a. Thing   b. Truth0
    c. Undefined   d. Undefined

148. A _____ is the sum of the elements of a sequence.

a. Thing
b. Series0
c. Undefined
d. Undefined

149. In geometry and physics, _____ are half-lines that continue forever in one direction.
a. Thing
b. Rays0
c. Undefined
d. Undefined

150. _____ is electromagnetic radiation with a wavelength that is visible to the eye (visible _____) or, in a technical or scientific context, electromagnetic radiation of any wavelength.
a. Thing
b. Light0
c. Undefined
d. Undefined

151. A _____ given two distinct points A and B on the _____, is the set of points C on the line containing points A and B such that A is not strictly between C and B.
a. Thing
b. Ray0
c. Undefined
d. Undefined

152. _____ is the state of being greater than any finite real or natural number, however large.
a. Thing
b. Infinite0
c. Undefined
d. Undefined

153. _____ is often represented as the sum of a sequence of terms.
a. Thing
b. Infinite series0
c. Undefined
d. Undefined

154. _____ is the study of geometry using the principles of algebra. _____ can be explained more simply: it is concerned with defining geometrical shapes in a numerical way and extracting numerical information from that representation.
a. Analytic geometry0
b. Thing
c. Undefined
d. Undefined

155. Sir _____ was an English physicist, mathematician, astronomer, natural philosopher, and alchemist, regarded by many as the greatest figure in the history of science.
a. Person
b. Isaac Newton0
c. Undefined
d. Undefined

156. In functional analysis and related areas of mathematics the _____ set of a given subset of a vector space is a certain set in the dual space.
a. Polar0
b. Thing
c. Undefined
d. Undefined

157. In mathematics, defined and _____ are used to explain whether or not expressions have meaningful, sensible, and unambiguous values.
a. Thing
b. Undefined0
c. Undefined
d. Undefined

Chapter 1. The Geometry of Euclidean Space

158. In classical geometry, a _____ of a circle or sphere is any line segment from its center to its boundary. By extension, the _____ of a circle or sphere is the length of any such segment. The _____ is half the diameter. In science and engineering the term _____ of curvature is commonly used as a synonym for _____.
   a. Thing
   b. Radius0
   c. Undefined
   d. Undefined

159. In mathematics, the _____ of a function is the set of all "output" values produced by that function. Given a function $f : A \to B$, the _____ of f, is defined to be the set $\{x \in B : x = f(a) \text{ for some } a \in A\}$.
   a. Thing
   b. Range0
   c. Undefined
   d. Undefined

160. In mathematics, a _____ is a quadric surface, with the following equation in Cartesian coordinates: $(x/_a)^2 + (y/_b)^2 = 1$.
   a. Thing
   b. Cylinder0
   c. Undefined
   d. Undefined

161. In mathematics, a _____ is a collection of points which share a property.
   a. Locus0
   b. Thing
   c. Undefined
   d. Undefined

162. In elementary algebra, an _____ is a set that contains every real number between two indicated numbers and may contain the two numbers themselves.
   a. Interval0
   b. Thing
   c. Undefined
   d. Undefined

163. _____ means "constancy", i.e. if something retains a certain feature even after we change a way of looking at it, then it is symmetric.
   a. Thing
   b. Symmetry0
   c. Undefined
   d. Undefined

164. In mathematics, a _____ is the set of all points in three-dimensional space (R^3) which are at distance r from a fixed point of that space, where r is a positive real number called the radius of the _____. The fixed point is called the center or centre, and is not part of the _____ itself.
   a. Thing
   b. Sphere0
   c. Undefined
   d. Undefined

165. An _____ is a type of quadric surface that is a higher dimensional analogue of an ellipse.
   a. Ellipsoid0
   b. Thing
   c. Undefined
   d. Undefined

166. _____, was an Italian mathematician and astronomer who created the calculus of variations which was later expanded by Weierstrass, solved the isoperimetrical problem on which the variational calculus is based in part.
   a. Joseph Louis Lagrange0
   b. Person
   c. Undefined
   d. Undefined

Chapter 1. The Geometry of Euclidean Space

167. The _____ of a function is an extension of the concept of a sum, and are identified or found through the use of integration.
 a. Integral0
 b. Thing
 c. Undefined
 d. Undefined

168. _____ is the process of planning, recording, and controlling the movement of a craft or vehicle from one place to another.
 a. Navigation0
 b. Thing
 c. Undefined
 d. Undefined

169. _____, usually denoted symbolically by the Greek letter phi, Î¦, gives the location of a place on Earth north or south of the equator. _____ is an angular measurement in degrees (marked with Â°) ranging from 0Â° at the Equator (low _____) to 90Â° at the poles (90Â° N for the North Pole or 90Â° S for the South Pole; high _____). The complementary angle of a _____ is called the colatitude.
 a. Thing
 b. Latitude0
 c. Undefined
 d. Undefined

170. _____ describes the location of a place on Earth east or west of a north-south line called the Prime Meridian.
 a. Thing
 b. Longitude0
 c. Undefined
 d. Undefined

171. A _____ is a function that assigns a number to subsets of a given set.
 a. Thing
 b. Measure0
 c. Undefined
 d. Undefined

172. In geometry, a _____ (Greek words diairo = divide and metro = measure) of a circle is any straight line segment that passes through the centre and whose endpoints are on the circular boundary, or, in more modern usage, the length of such a line segment. When using the word in the more modern sense, one speaks of the _____ rather than a _____, because all diameters of a circle have the same length. This length is twice the radius. The _____ of a circle is also the longest chord that the circle has.
 a. Diameter0
 b. Thing
 c. Undefined
 d. Undefined

173. In mathematics, the concept of a _____ tries to capture the intuitive idea of a geometrical one-dimensional and continuous object. A simple example is the circle.
 a. Thing
 b. Curve0
 c. Undefined
 d. Undefined

174. The _____ of an angle is the ratio of the length of the adjacent side to the length of the hypotenuse.
 a. Cosine0
 b. Concept
 c. Undefined
 d. Undefined

175. _____ is bother the congnitive process of transferring information from a particular subject , and a linguistic expression corresponding to such a process.

Chapter 1. The Geometry of Euclidean Space

a. Thing
b. Analogy0
c. Undefined
d. Undefined

176. The _____ is a statement about a general triangle which relates the lengths of its sides to the cosine of one of its angles.
    a. Law of cosines0
    b. Thing
    c. Undefined
    d. Undefined

177. A _____ is a negotiable instrument instructing a financial institution to pay a specific amount of a specific currency from a specific demand account held in the maker/depositor's name with that institution. Both the maker and payee may be natural persons or legal entities.
    a. Thing
    b. Check0
    c. Undefined
    d. Undefined

178. A _____ is 360° or 2δ radians.
    a. Turn0
    b. Thing
    c. Undefined
    d. Undefined

179. The word _____ comes from the Latin word linearis, which means created by lines.
    a. Thing
    b. Linear0
    c. Undefined
    d. Undefined

180. In mathematics, a _____ in elementary terms is any of a variety of different functions from geometry, such as rotations, reflections and translations.
    a. Thing
    b. Transformation0
    c. Undefined
    d. Undefined

181. In mathematics, a linear map also called a _____ or linear operator is a function between two vector spaces that preserves the operations of vector addition and scalar multiplication.
    a. Thing
    b. Linear transformation0
    c. Undefined
    d. Undefined

182. _____ element of an element x with respect to a binary operation * with identity element e is an element y such that x * y = y * x = e. In particular,
    a. Thing
    b. Inverse0
    c. Undefined
    d. Undefined

183. In mathematics, the idea of _____ generalises the concepts of negation, in relation to addition, and reciprocal, in relation to multiplication.
    a. Inverse element0
    b. Thing
    c. Undefined
    d. Undefined

184. The Gaussian _____ is an algorithm which can be used to determine the solutions of a system of linear equations, to find the rank of a matrix, and to calculate the inverse of an invertible square matrix.

Chapter 1. The Geometry of Euclidean Space

a. Thing
b. Elimination method0
c. Undefined
d. Undefined

185. In statistics, a _____ measure is one which is measuring what is supposed to measure.
a. Thing
b. Valid0
c. Undefined
d. Undefined

186. _____ was a highly influential French philosopher, mathematician, scientist, and writer. Dubbed the "Founder of Modern Philosophy", and the "Father of Modern Mathematics". His theories provided the basis for the calculus of Newton and Leibniz, by applying infinitesimal calculus to the tangent line problem, thus permitting the evolution of that branch of modern mathematics
a. Person
b. Descartes0
c. Undefined
d. Undefined

187. In mathematics and logic, a _____ proof is a way of showing the truth or falsehood of a given statement by a straightforward combination of established facts, usually existing lemmas and theorems, without making any further assumptions.
a. Direct0
b. Thing
c. Undefined
d. Undefined

188. The _____ of a ring R is defined to be the smallest positive integer n such that $n\,a = 0$, for all a in R.
a. Thing
b. Characteristic0
c. Undefined
d. Undefined

189. An _____ or member of a set is an object that when collected together make up the set.
a. Element0
b. Thing
c. Undefined
d. Undefined

190. In mathematics, the _____ , or members of a set or more generally a class are all those objects which when collected together make up the set or class.
a. Thing
b. Elements0
c. Undefined
d. Undefined

191. In mathematics, _____ refers to a number of loosely related concepts in different areas of geometry. Intuitively, _____ is the amount by which a geometric object deviates from being flat, but this is defined in different ways depending on the context
a. Curvature0
b. Thing
c. Undefined
d. Undefined

192. In mathematics a _____ is a function which defines a distance between elements of a set.
a. Metric0
b. Thing
c. Undefined
d. Undefined

193. A _____ is an abstract model that uses mathematical language to describe the behavior of a system. Eykhoff defined a _____ as 'a representation of the essential aspects of an existing system which presents knowledge of that system in usable form'.

Chapter 1. The Geometry of Euclidean Space

    a. Thing   b. Mathematical model0
    c. Undefined   d. Undefined

194. _____ was a British mathematician. He helped found the modern British school of pure mathematics.
    a. Person   b. Arthur Cayley0
    c. Undefined   d. Undefined

195. _____ is a collection of objects called vectors that, informally speaking, may be scaled and added.
    a. Thing   b. Vector space0
    c. Undefined   d. Undefined

196. _____ was a German mathematician. Although much of his working life was spent in Zürich and then Princeton, he is closely identified with the University of Göttingen tradition of mathematics, represented by David Hilbert and Hermann Minkowski. His research has had major significance for theoretical physics as well as pure disciplines including number theory. He was one of the most influential mathematicians of the twentieth century, and a key member of the Institute for Advanced Study in its early years, in terms of creating an integrated and international view.
    a. Hermann Weyl0   b. Person
    c. Undefined   d. Undefined

197. A _____ function is a function for which, intuitively, small changes in the input result in small changes in the output
    a. Continuous0   b. Event
    c. Undefined   d. Undefined

198. _____ is the property of a physical object that quantifies the amount of matter and energy it is equivalent to.
    a. Thing   b. Mass0
    c. Undefined   d. Undefined

199. The metre (or _____, see spelling differences) is a measure of length. It is the basic unit of length in the metric system and in the International System of Units (SI), used around the world for general and scientific purposes.
    a. Meter0   b. Concept
    c. Undefined   d. Undefined

200. A _____ (plural: tetrahedra) is a polyhedron composed of four triangular faces, three of which meet at each vertex.
    a. Thing   b. Tetrahedron0
    c. Undefined   d. Undefined

201. In geometry, three or more lines are said to be _____ if they intersect at a single point.
    a. Thing   b. Concurrent0
    c. Undefined   d. Undefined

202. In geometry, the _____ of an object is a point in some sense in the middle of the object.
    a. Thing   b. Center0
    c. Undefined   d. Undefined

203. In physics, the _____ of a system of particles is a specific point at which, for many purposes, the system's mass behaves as if it were concentrated.
   a. Thing
   b. Center of mass0
   c. Undefined
   d. Undefined

Chapter 2. Differentiation

1. A _____ signifies a point or points of probability on a subject e.g., the _____ of creativity, which allows for the formation of rule or norm or law by interpretation of the phenomena events that can be created.
   a. Principle0
   b. Thing
   c. Undefined
   d. Undefined

2. A _____ is a symbolic representation denoting a quantity or expression. It often represents an "unknown" quantity that has the potential to change.
   a. Thing
   b. Variable0
   c. Undefined
   d. Undefined

3. _____ is a mathematical subject that includes the study of limits, derivatives, integrals, and power series and constitutes a major part of modern university curriculum.
   a. Thing
   b. Calculus0
   c. Undefined
   d. Undefined

4. A _____ is traditionally an infinitesimally small change in a variable.
   a. Thing
   b. Differential0
   c. Undefined
   d. Undefined

5. _____, a field in mathematics, is the study of how functions change when their inputs change. The primary object of study in _____ is the derivative.
   a. Thing
   b. Differential calculus0
   c. Undefined
   d. Undefined

6. The mathematical concept of a _____ expresses the intuitive idea of deterministic dependence between two quantities, one of which is viewed as primary and the other as secondary. A _____ then is a way to associate a unique output for each input of a specified type, for example, a real number or an element of a given set.
   a. Function0
   b. Thing
   c. Undefined
   d. Undefined

7. In mathematics, a _____ is the result of multiplying, or an expression that identifies factors to be multiplied.
   a. Thing
   b. Product0
   c. Undefined
   d. Undefined

8. In mathematics, a _____ is the end result of a division problem. It can also be expressed as the number of times the divisor divides into the dividend.
   a. Quotient0
   b. Thing
   c. Undefined
   d. Undefined

9. A _____ is the result of the addition of a set of numbers. The numbers may be natural numbers, complex numbers, matrices, or still more complicated objects. An infinite _____ is a subtle procedure known as a series.
   a. Sum0
   b. Thing
   c. Undefined
   d. Undefined

10. In mathematics, a _____ of a positive integer n is a way of writing n as a sum of positive integers.

Chapter 2. Differentiation   25

a. Composition0   b. Thing
c. Undefined   d. Undefined

11. The _____ is a measurement of how a function changes when the values of its inputs change.
a. Derivative0   b. Thing
c. Undefined   d. Undefined

12. In mathematics, a _____ is a demonstration that, assuming certain axioms, some statement is necessarily true.
a. Proof0   b. Thing
c. Undefined   d. Undefined

13. Mathematical _____ are demonstrations that, assuming certain axioms, some statement is necessarily true.
a. Thing   b. Proofs0
c. Undefined   d. Undefined

14. In trigonometry, the _____ is a function defined as $\tan x = \sin x / \cos x$. The function is so-named because it can be defined as the length of a certain segment of a _____ (in the geometric sense) to the unit circle. In plane geometry, a line is _____ to a curve, at some point, if both line and curve pass through the point with the same direction.
a. Tangent0   b. Thing
c. Undefined   d. Undefined

15. In mathematics, a _____ is a two-dimensional manifold or surface that is perfectly flat.
a. Thing   b. Plane0
c. Undefined   d. Undefined

16. In mathematics, _____ are two-dimensional manifolds or surfaces that are perfectly flat.
a. Thing   b. Planes0
c. Undefined   d. Undefined

17. In mathematics, a _____ is a rectangular table of numbers or, more generally, a table consisting of abstract quantities that can be added and multiplied.
a. Matrix0   b. Thing
c. Undefined   d. Undefined

18. _____ is a branch of mathematics concerning the study of structure, relation and quantity.
a. Algebra0   b. Concept
c. Undefined   d. Undefined

19. In physics and in _____ calculus, a spatial _____, or simply _____, is a concept characterized by a magnitude and a direction.
a. Thing   b. Vector0
c. Undefined   d. Undefined

20. Mathematical _____ is used to represent ideas.

a. Thing
b. Notation0
c. Undefined
d. Undefined

21. In mathematics, the _____ of a function is the set of all "output" values produced by that function. Given a function $f : A \to B$, the _____ of f, is defined to be the set $\{x \in B : x = f(a) \text{ for some } a \in A\}$.

a. Thing
b. Range0
c. Undefined
d. Undefined

22. A _____ is a set whose members are members of another set or a set contained within another set.

a. Thing
b. Subset0
c. Undefined
d. Undefined

23. A _____, is a symbolized depiction of space which highlights relations between components of that space. Most usually a _____ is a two-dimensional, geometrically accurate representation of a three-dimensional space.

a. Thing
b. Map0
c. Undefined
d. Undefined

24. The _____, the average in everyday English, which is also called the arithmetic _____ (and is distinguished from the geometric _____ or harmonic _____). The average is also called the sample _____. The expected value of a random variable, which is also called the population _____.

a. Thing
b. Mean0
c. Undefined
d. Undefined

25. In linear algebra, real numbers are called scalars and relate to vectors in a vector space through the operation of _____ multiplication, in which a vector can be multiplied by a number to produce another vector.

a. Scalar0
b. Thing
c. Undefined
d. Undefined

26. In mathematics, a _____ of a k-place relation $L \subseteq X_1 \times \ldots \times X_k$ is one of the sets X_j, $1 \leq j \leq k$. In the special case where k = 2 and $L \subseteq X_1 \times X_2$ is a function $L : X_1 \to X_2$, it is conventional to refer to X_1 as the _____ of the function and to refer to X_2 as the codomain of the function.

a. Thing
b. Domain0
c. Undefined
d. Undefined

27. _____, verti-bar, vertical line, divider line, or pipe is the name of the character .

a. Vertical bar0
b. Thing
c. Undefined
d. Undefined

28. In mathematics, the _____ f is the collection of all ordered pairs . In particular, graph means the graphical representation of this collection, in the form of a curve or surface, together with axes, etc. Graphing on a Cartesian plane is sometimes referred to as curve sketching.

a. Graph of a function0
b. Thing
c. Undefined
d. Undefined

29. _____ are the basic objects of study in graph theory. Informally speaking, a graph is a set of objects called points, nodes, or vertices connected by links called lines or edges.

a. Graphs0 b. Thing
c. Undefined d. Undefined

30. _____ are objects, characters, or other concrete representations of ideas, concepts, or other abstractions.
a. Symbols0 b. Thing
c. Undefined d. Undefined

31. In mathematics, the concept of a _____ tries to capture the intuitive idea of a geometrical one-dimensional and continuous object. A simple example is the circle.
a. Thing b. Curve0
c. Undefined d. Undefined

32. The _____ (symbol _____) and the millibar (symbol mbar, also mb) are units of pressure.
a. Thing b. Bar0
c. Undefined d. Undefined

33. In mathematics, _____ are the intuitive idea of a geometrical one-dimensional and continuous object.
a. Curves0 b. Thing
c. Undefined d. Undefined

34. A _____ is a map illustrated with contour lines, for example a topographic map.
a. Thing b. Contour map0
c. Undefined d. Undefined

35. In geometry, an _____ of a triangle is a straight line through a vertex and perpendicular to (i.e. forming a right angle with) the opposite side or an extension of the opposite side.
a. Altitude0 b. Concept
c. Undefined d. Undefined

36. In mathematics and the mathematical sciences, a _____ is a fixed, but possibly unspecified, value. This is in contrast to a variable, which is not fixed.
a. Constant0 b. Thing
c. Undefined d. Undefined

37. In mathematical analysis, a _____ is a classification of functions according to the properties of their derivatives.
a. Thing b. Smooth surface0
c. Undefined d. Undefined

38. _____ is a set, with some particular properties and usually some additional structure, such as the operations of addition or multiplication, for instance.
a. Space0 b. Thing
c. Undefined d. Undefined

39. In Euclidean geometry, a _____ is the set of all points in a plane at a fixed distance, called the radius, from a given point, the center.

a. Circle0
b. Thing
c. Undefined
d. Undefined

40. In mathematics and more specifically set theory, the _____ set is the unique set which contains no elements.
    a. Empty0
    b. Thing
    c. Undefined
    d. Undefined

41. In classical geometry, a _____ of a circle or sphere is any line segment from its center to its boundary. By extension, the _____ of a circle or sphere is the length of any such segment. The _____ is half the diameter. In science and engineering the term _____ of curvature is commonly used as a synonym for _____.
    a. Radius0
    b. Thing
    c. Undefined
    d. Undefined

42. In mathematics, the _____ of a coordinate system is the point where the axes of the system intersect.
    a. Origin0
    b. Thing
    c. Undefined
    d. Undefined

43. A _____ is a polynomial function of the form $f(x) = ax^2 + bx + c$, where a, b, c are real numbers and a , 0.
    a. Event
    b. Quadratic function0
    c. Undefined
    d. Undefined

44. _____ is a quadric
    a. Thing
    b. Paraboloid0
    c. Undefined
    d. Undefined

45. _____ is a quadric, a type of surface in three dimensions
    a. Hyperbolic paraboloid0
    b. Thing
    c. Undefined
    d. Undefined

46. An _____ is a straight line around which a geometric figure can be rotated.
    a. Thing
    b. Axis0
    c. Undefined
    d. Undefined

47. In mathematics, a _____ is a type of conic section defined as the intersection between a right circular conical surface and a plane which cuts through both halves of the cone.
    a. Hyperbola0
    b. Thing
    c. Undefined
    d. Undefined

48. In mathematics, a _____ is the set of all points in three-dimensional space (R^3) which are at distance r from a fixed point of that space, where r is a positive real number called the radius of the _____. The fixed point is called the center or centre, and is not part of the _____ itself.
    a. Sphere0
    b. Thing
    c. Undefined
    d. Undefined

49. A _____ is a three-dimensional geometric shape formed by straight lines through a fixed point (vertex) to the points of a fixed curve (directrix)

Chapter 2. Differentiation

    a. Cone0
    b. Concept
    c. Undefined
    d. Undefined

50. A _____ is a set of numbers that designate location in a given reference system, such as x,y in a planar _____ system or an x,y,z in a three-dimensional _____ system.
    a. Thing
    b. Coordinate0
    c. Undefined
    d. Undefined

51. In functional analysis and related areas of mathematics the _____ set of a given subset of a vector space is a certain set in the dual space.
    a. Thing
    b. Polar0
    c. Undefined
    d. Undefined

52. In mathematics, a _____ may be described informally as a number that can be given by an infinite decimal representation.
    a. Real number0
    b. Thing
    c. Undefined
    d. Undefined

53. In geometry, the _____ of an object is a point in some sense in the middle of the object.
    a. Thing
    b. Center0
    c. Undefined
    d. Undefined

54. In mathematics, an _____ is a statement about the relative size or order of two objects.
    a. Inequality0
    b. Thing
    c. Undefined
    d. Undefined

55. In elementary algebra, an _____ is a set that contains every real number between two indicated numbers and may contain the two numbers themselves.
    a. Interval0
    b. Thing
    c. Undefined
    d. Undefined

56. An _____ or member of a set is an object that when collected together make up the set.
    a. Thing
    b. Element0
    c. Undefined
    d. Undefined

57. In mathematics, the _____ , or members of a set or more generally a class are all those objects which when collected together make up the set or class.
    a. Thing
    b. Elements0
    c. Undefined
    d. Undefined

58. In mathematics and more specifically set theory, the _____ is the unique set which contains no elements.
    a. Thing
    b. Empty set0
    c. Undefined
    d. Undefined

59. In mathematics, a _____ is a statement that can be proved on the basis of explicitly stated or previously agreed assumptions.

Chapter 2. Differentiation

    a. Theorem0
    b. Thing
    c. Undefined
    d. Undefined

60. A _____ is 360° or 2∂ radians.
    a. Turn0
    b. Thing
    c. Undefined
    d. Undefined

61. The plus and _____ signs are mathematical symbols used to represent the notions of positive and negative as well as the operations of addition and subtraction.
    a. Thing
    b. Minus0
    c. Undefined
    d. Undefined

62. _____ Any process by which a specified characteristic usually amplitude of the output of a device is prevented from exceeding a predetermined value.
    a. Thing
    b. Limiting0
    c. Undefined
    d. Undefined

63. An _____ is a combination of numbers, operators, grouping symbols and/or free variables and bound variables arranged in a meaningful way which can be evaluated..
    a. Expression0
    b. Thing
    c. Undefined
    d. Undefined

64. A _____ function is a function for which, intuitively, small changes in the input result in small changes in the output.
    a. Event
    b. Continuous0
    c. Undefined
    d. Undefined

65. Continuous functions are of utmost importance in mathematics and applications. However, not all functions are continuous. If a function is not continuous at a point in its domain, one says that it has a _____ there. The set of all points of _____ of a function may be a discrete set, a dense set, or even the entire domain of the function.
    a. Discontinuity0
    b. Thing
    c. Undefined
    d. Undefined

66. In mathematics, in the field of group theory, a _____ of a group is a quasisimple subnormal subgroup.
    a. Component0
    b. Concept
    c. Undefined
    d. Undefined

67. In mathematics, _____ is a part of the set theoretic notion of function.
    a. Image0
    b. Thing
    c. Undefined
    d. Undefined

68. A _____ is a deliberate process for transforming one or more inputs into one or more results.
    a. Thing
    b. Calculation0
    c. Undefined
    d. Undefined

69. In statistics, a _____ measure is one which is measuring what is supposed to measure.

Chapter 2. Differentiation 31

   a. Thing   b. Valid0
   c. Undefined   d. Undefined

70. In a mathematical proof or a syllogism, a _____ is a statement that is the logical consequence of preceding statements.
   a. Concept   b. Conclusion0
   c. Undefined   d. Undefined

71. _____ element of an element x with respect to a binary operation * with identity element e is an element y such that x * y = y * x = e. In particular,
   a. Thing   b. Inverse0
   c. Undefined   d. Undefined

72. In geographic information systems, a _____ comprises an entity with a geographic location, typically determined by points, arcs, or polygons. Carriageways and cadastres exemplify _____ data.
   a. Thing   b. Feature0
   c. Undefined   d. Undefined

73. A _____ is a special kind of ratio, indicating a relationship between two measurements with different units, such as miles to gallons or cents to pounds.
   a. Rate0   b. Thing
   c. Undefined   d. Undefined

74. _____ is a free computer algebra system based on a 1982 version of Macsyma
   a. Maxima0   b. Thing
   c. Undefined   d. Undefined

75. _____ are points in the domain of a function at which the function takes a largest value or smallest value, either within a given neighborhood or on the function domain in its entirety.
   a. Thing   b. Maxima and minima0
   c. Undefined   d. Undefined

76. In mathematics, maxima and _____, known collectively as extrema, are points in the domain of a function at which the function takes a largest value .
   a. Thing   b. Minima0
   c. Undefined   d. Undefined

77. _____ of a function of several variables is its derivative with respect to one of those variables with the others held constant as opposed to the total derivative, in which all variables are allowed to vary.
   a. Thing   b. Partial derivative0
   c. Undefined   d. Undefined

78. In mathematics, _____ notation occurs when an author uses a mathematical notation in a way that is not formally correct but that seems likely to simplify the exposition .

a. Abuse of0
b. Thing
c. Undefined
d. Undefined

79. The _____ is a method of finding the derivative of a function that is the quotient of two other functions for which derivatives exist.
   a. Thing
   b. Quotient rule0
   c. Undefined
   d. Undefined

80. In calculus, the _____ is a formula for the derivative of the composite of two functions.
   a. Concept
   b. Chain rule0
   c. Undefined
   d. Undefined

81. A _____ number is a positive integer which has a positive divisor other than one or itself.
   a. Composite0
   b. Thing
   c. Undefined
   d. Undefined

82. A _____ consists of one quarter of the coordinate plane.
   a. Quadrant0
   b. Thing
   c. Undefined
   d. Undefined

83. _____ is often used to describe the measurement of the steepness, incline, gradient, or grade of a straight line. The _____ is defined as the ratio of the "rise" divided by the "run" between two points on a line, or in other words, the ratio of the altitude change to the horizontal distance between any two points on the line.
   a. Slope0
   b. Thing
   c. Undefined
   d. Undefined

84. An _____ is when two lines intersect somewhere on a plane creating a right angle at intersection
   a. Thing
   b. Axes0
   c. Undefined
   d. Undefined

85. _____ has two distinct but etymologically-related meanings: one in geometry and one in trigonometry.
   a. Thing
   b. Tangent line0
   c. Undefined
   d. Undefined

86. The word _____ comes from the Latin word linearis, which means created by lines.
   a. Thing
   b. Linear0
   c. Undefined
   d. Undefined

87. _____ is an approximation of a general function using a linear function more precisely, an affine function.
   a. Linear approximation0
   b. Thing
   c. Undefined
   d. Undefined

88. In linear algebra, the _____ of an n-by-n square matrix A is defined to be the sum of the elements on the main diagonal of A,

Chapter 2. Differentiation 33

   a. Thing
   c. Undefined
   b. Trace0
   d. Undefined

89. In mathematics, an _____ is any of the arguments, i.e. "inputs", to a function. Thus if we have a function f(x), then x is a _____.
   a. Independent variable0
   b. Thing
   c. Undefined
   d. Undefined

90. _____ is a circle with a unit radius, i.e., a circle whose radius is 1.
   a. Unit circle0
   b. Thing
   c. Undefined
   d. Undefined

91. Initial objects are also called _____, and terminal objects are also called final.
   a. Coterminal0
   b. Thing
   c. Undefined
   d. Undefined

92. _____ of an object is its speed in a particular direction.
   a. Velocity0
   b. Thing
   c. Undefined
   d. Undefined

93. The _____ is the distance around a closed curve. _____ is a kind of perimeter.
   a. Circumference0
   b. Thing
   c. Undefined
   d. Undefined

94. A _____ is the curve defined by the path of a point on the edge of circular wheel as the wheel rolls along a straight line.
   a. Thing
   b. Cycloid0
   c. Undefined
   d. Undefined

95. A _____ is a movement of an object in a circular motion. A two-dimensional object rotates around a center (or point) of _____. A three-dimensional object rotates around a line called an axis. If the axis of _____ is within the body, the body is said to rotate upon itself, or spin—which implies relative speed and perhaps free-movement with angular momentum. A circular motion about an external point, e.g. the Earth about the Sun, is called an orbit or more properly an orbital revolution.
   a. Rotation0
   b. Thing
   c. Undefined
   d. Undefined

96. In physics, the _____ momentum of an object rotating about some reference point is the measure of the extent to which the object will continue to rotate about that point unless acted upon by an external torque.
   a. Thing
   b. Angular0
   c. Undefined
   d. Undefined

97. In physics, the _____ is a vector quantity (more precisely, a pseudovector) which specifies the angular speed at which an object is rotating along with the direction in which it is rotating.

Chapter 2. Differentiation

a. Angular velocity0
b. Thing
c. Undefined
d. Undefined

98. _____ is a plane curve produced by tracing the path of a chosen point of a circle — called epicycle — which rolls without slipping around a fixed circle. It is a particular kind of roulette.
   a. Thing
   b. Epicycloid0
   c. Undefined
   d. Undefined

99. Blaise _____ was a French mathematician, physicist, and religious philosopher.
   a. Pascal0
   b. Person
   c. Undefined
   d. Undefined

100. _____ was a French mathematician, physicist, and religious philosopher.
   a. Person
   b. Blaise Pascal0
   c. Undefined
   d. Undefined

101. A _____ is an object that is attached to a pivot point so that it can swing freely.
   a. Pendulum0
   b. Thing
   c. Undefined
   d. Undefined

102. Compass and straightedge or ruler-and-compass _____ is the _____ of lengths or angles using only an idealized ruler and compass.
   a. Construction0
   b. Thing
   c. Undefined
   d. Undefined

103. In geometry, an _____ is a point at which a line segment or ray terminates.
   a. Endpoint0
   b. Thing
   c. Undefined
   d. Undefined

104. In mathematics, a _____ is a quadric surface, with the following equation in Cartesian coordinates: $(x/_a)^2 + (y/_b)^2 = 1$.
   a. Cylinder0
   b. Thing
   c. Undefined
   d. Undefined

105. A _____ of a number is the product of that number with any integer.
   a. Multiple0
   b. Thing
   c. Undefined
   d. Undefined

106. _____ statistics are statistics that estimate population parameters.
   a. Thing
   b. Parametric0
   c. Undefined
   d. Undefined

107. A _____, formed by the composition of one function on another, represents the application of the former to the result of the application of the latter to the argument of the composite.

Chapter 2. Differentiation

a. Thing
b. Composite function0
c. Undefined
d. Undefined

108. A _____ is one of the basic shapes of geometry: a polygon with three vertices and three sides which are straight line segments.
a. Triangle0
b. Thing
c. Undefined
d. Undefined

109. _____ is the theorem stating that for any triangle, the measure of a given side must be less than the sum of the other two sides but greater than the difference between the two sides.
a. Triangle inequality0
b. Thing
c. Undefined
d. Undefined

110. In mathematics and logic, a _____ proof is a way of showing the truth or falsehood of a given statement by a straightforward combination of established facts, usually existing lemmas and theorems, without making any further assumptions.
a. Thing
b. Direct0
c. Undefined
d. Undefined

111. Equivalence is the condition of being _____ or essentially equal.
a. Equivalent0
b. Thing
c. Undefined
d. Undefined

112. In mathematics, science including computer science, linguistics and engineering, an _____ is, generally speaking, an independent variable or input to a function.
a. Argument0
b. Thing
c. Undefined
d. Undefined

113. In common philosophical language, a proposition or _____, is the content of an assertion, that is, it is true-or-false and defined by the meaning of a particular piece of language.
a. Concept
b. Statement0
c. Undefined
d. Undefined

114. In mathematics, _____ is an elementary arithmetic operation. When one of the numbers is a whole number, _____ is the repeated sum of the other number.
a. Multiplication0
b. Thing
c. Undefined
d. Undefined

115. _____ is a trigonemtric function that is important when studying triangles and modeling periodic phenomena, among other applications.
a. Sine0
b. Thing
c. Undefined
d. Undefined

116. A _____ is a negotiable instrument instructing a financial institution to pay a specific amount of a specific currency from a specific demand account held in the maker/depositor's name with that institution. Both the maker and payee may be natural persons or legal entities.

a. Thing
b. Check0
c. Undefined
d. Undefined

117. _____ is a branch of physics that studies the effects of changes in temperature, pressure, and volume on physical systems at the macroscopic scale by analyzing the collective motion of their particles using statistics.
a. Thing
b. Thermodynamics0
c. Undefined
d. Undefined

118. The _____ of a solid object is the three-dimensional concept of how much space it occupies, often quantified numerically.
a. Volume0
b. Thing
c. Undefined
d. Undefined

119. _____ is a physical property of a system that underlies the common notions of hot and cold; something that is hotter has the greater _____.
a. Thing
b. Temperature0
c. Undefined
d. Undefined

120. A _____ fraction is a fraction in which the absolute value of the numerator is less than the denominator--hence, the absolute value of the fraction is less than 1.
a. Proper0
b. Thing
c. Undefined
d. Undefined

121. The term _____, or axiom, indicates a starting assumption from which other statements are logically derived.
a. Thing
b. Postulate0
c. Undefined
d. Undefined

122. In chemistry, a _____ is substance made by combining two or more different materials in such a way that no chemical reaction occurs.
a. Thing
b. Mixture0
c. Undefined
d. Undefined

123. In vector calculus, the _____ of a scalar field is a vector field which points in the direction of the greatest rate of increase of the scalar field, and whose magnitude is the greatest rate of change.
a. Thing
b. Gradient0
c. Undefined
d. Undefined

124. _____ in a normed vector space is a vector whose length, or magnitude is 1.
a. Unit vector0
b. Thing
c. Undefined
d. Undefined

125. In mathematics, there are several meanings of _____ depending on the subject.
a. Degree0
b. Thing
c. Undefined
d. Undefined

Chapter 2. Differentiation

126. The metre (or _____, see spelling differences) is a measure of length. It is the basic unit of length in the metric system and in the International System of Units (SI), used around the world for general and scientific purposes.
   a. Meter0
   b. Concept
   c. Undefined
   d. Undefined

127. In geometry, two lines or planes if one falls on the other in such a way as to create congruent adjacent angles. The term may be used as a noun or adjective. Thus, referring to Figure 1, the line AB is the _____ to CD through the point B.
   a. Thing
   b. Perpendicular0
   c. Undefined
   d. Undefined

128. In mathematics, _____ is synonymous with perpendicular when used as a simple adjective that is not part of any longer phrase with a standard definition. It means at right angles. It comes from the Greek á½€Ï Î¸ÏŒÏ, orthos, meaning "straight", used by Euclid to mean right; and Î³Ï‰Î½Î¯Î± gonia, meaning angle. Two streets that cross each other at a right angle are _____ to one another.
   a. Orthogonal0
   b. Thing
   c. Undefined
   d. Undefined

129. A _____ consists either of a suggested explanation for a phenomenon or of a reasoned proposal suggesting a possible correlation between multiple phenomena.
   a. Thing
   b. Hypothesis0
   c. Undefined
   d. Undefined

130. _____ is a construction in vector calculus which associates a vector to every point in a locally Euclidean space.
   a. Thing
   b. Vector field0
   c. Undefined
   d. Undefined

131. Sir Isaac _____, was an English physicist, mathematician, astronomer, natural philosopher, and alchemist, regarded by many as the greatest figure in the history of science
   a. Newton0
   b. Person
   c. Undefined
   d. Undefined

132. _____ is the weakest of the four fundamental forces of bature, as described by Issac Newton
   a. Thing
   b. Gravitational force0
   c. Undefined
   d. Undefined

133. Isaac Newton's _____ states the following:Every single point mass attracts every other point mass by a force pointing along the line combining the two.
   a. Thing
   b. Law of gravitation0
   c. Undefined
   d. Undefined

134. _____ is the property of a physical object that quantifies the amount of matter and energy it is equivalent to.
   a. Thing
   b. Mass0
   c. Undefined
   d. Undefined

135. In physics, a _____ may refer to the scalar _____ or to the vector _____.

a. Potential0
b. Thing
c. Undefined
d. Undefined

136. In physics, _____ is an influence that may cause an object to accelerate. It may be experienced as a lift, a push, or a pull. The actual acceleration of the body is determined by the vector sum of all forces acting on it, known as net _____ or resultant _____.
    a. Force0
    b. Thing
    c. Undefined
    d. Undefined

137. In mathematics, an inequality is a statement about the relative size or order of two objects. For example 14 > 10, or 14 is _____ 10.
    a. Thing
    b. Greater than0
    c. Undefined
    d. Undefined

138. _____ are functions which satisfy particular symmetry relations, with respect to taking additive inverses.
    a. Thing
    b. Even function0
    c. Undefined
    d. Undefined

139. A _____ is a landform that extends above the surrounding terrain in a limited area. A _____ is generally steeper than a hill, but there is no universally accepted standard definition for the height of a _____ or a hill although a _____ usually has an identifiable summit.
    a. Thing
    b. Mountain0
    c. Undefined
    d. Undefined

140. _____ has many meanings, most of which simply .
    a. Thing
    b. Power0
    c. Undefined
    d. Undefined

141. In mathematics, the additive inverse, or _____ of a number n is the number that, when added to n, yields zero. The additive inverse of n is denoted −n. For example, 7 is −7, because 7 + (−7) = 0, and the additive inverse of −0.3 is 0.3, because −0.3 + 0.3 = 0.
    a. Opposite0
    b. Thing
    c. Undefined
    d. Undefined

142. In mathematics, the _____ of a number n is the number that, when added to n, yields zero. The _____ of n is denoted −n. For example, 7 is −7, because 7 + (−7) = 0, and the _____ of −0.3 is 0.3, because −0.3 + 0.3 = 0.
    a. Additive inverse0
    b. Thing
    c. Undefined
    d. Undefined

143. In astronomy, geography, geometry and related sciences and contexts, a plane is said to be _____ at a given point if it is locally perpendicular to the gradient of the gravity field, i.e., with the direction of the gravitational force at that point.
    a. Thing
    b. Horizontal0
    c. Undefined
    d. Undefined

144. In mathamatics, a _____ is a quadric, a type of surface in three dimensions, described by the equation

Chapter 2. Differentiation 39

a. Hyperboloid0
b. Thing
c. Undefined
d. Undefined

145. Leonhard _____ was a pioneering Swiss mathematician and physicist, who spent most of his life in Russia and Germany.
a. Euler0
b. Person
c. Undefined
d. Undefined

146. An _____ is an equality that remains true regardless of the values of any variables that appear within it, to distinguish it from an equality which is true under more particular conditions.
a. Identity0
b. Thing
c. Undefined
d. Undefined

147. A real-valued function f defined on the real line is said to have a _____ point at the point x∗, if there exists some ε > 0, such that f when x − x∗ < ε.
a. Thing
b. Local maximum0
c. Undefined
d. Undefined

148. One of the three formats applicable to a quadratic function is the _____ which is defined as $f = ax^2 + bx + c$.
a. General form0
b. Thing
c. Undefined
d. Undefined

149. The _____ of measurement are a globally standardized and modernized form of the metric system.
a. Thing
b. Units0
c. Undefined
d. Undefined

150. The _____ are a set of laws that describe the relationship between thermodynamic temperature T, pressure P and volume V of gases.
a. Thing
b. Gas law0
c. Undefined
d. Undefined

151. A _____ is a function that assigns a number to subsets of a given set.
a. Thing
b. Measure0
c. Undefined
d. Undefined

152. A _____ is a unit of length, usually used to measure distance, in a number of different systems, including Imperial units, United States customary units and Norwegian/Swedish mil. Its size can vary from system to system, but in each is between 1 and 10 kilometers. In contemporary English contexts _____ refers to either:
a. Mile0
b. Thing
c. Undefined
d. Undefined

Chapter 3. Higher-Order Derivatives; Maxima and Minima

1. Leonhard _____ was a pioneering Swiss mathematician and physicist, who spent most of his life in Russia and Germany.
   a. Euler0
   b. Person
   c. Undefined
   d. Undefined

2. _____ was a pioneering Swiss mathematician and physicist, who spent most of his life in Russia and Germany.
   a. Person
   b. Leonhard Euler0
   c. Undefined
   d. Undefined

3. _____ is a free computer algebra system based on a 1982 version of Macsyma
   a. Thing
   b. Maxima0
   c. Undefined
   d. Undefined

4. _____ are points in the domain of a function at which the function takes a largest value or smallest value, either within a given neighborhood or on the function domain in its entirety.
   a. Maxima and minima0
   b. Thing
   c. Undefined
   d. Undefined

5. The _____ is a measurement of how a function changes when the values of its inputs change.
   a. Thing
   b. Derivative0
   c. Undefined
   d. Undefined

6. In mathematics, maxima and _____, known collectively as extrema, are points in the domain of a function at which the function takes a largest value.
   a. Thing
   b. Minima0
   c. Undefined
   d. Undefined

7. The _____ is defined as the summation of all particles and energy that exist and the space-time which all events occur.
   a. Universe0
   b. Thing
   c. Undefined
   d. Undefined

8. The population _____ is the total number of human beings alive on the planet Earth at a given time.
   a. Thing
   b. Of the world0
   c. Undefined
   d. Undefined

9. A real-valued function f defined on the real line is said to have a _____ point at the point x∗, if there exists some ε > 0, such that f when x − x∗ < ε.
   a. Local maximum0
   b. Thing
   c. Undefined
   d. Undefined

10. Acid _____ ratio measures the ability of a company to use its near cash or quick assets to immediately extinguish its current liabilities.
    a. Thing
    b. Test0
    c. Undefined
    d. Undefined

Chapter 3. Higher-Order Derivatives; Maxima and Minima

11. _____ is a mathematical subject that includes the study of limits, derivatives, integrals, and power series and constitutes a major part of modern university curriculum.
   a. Thing
   b. Calculus0
   c. Undefined
   d. Undefined

12. The mathematical concept of a _____ expresses the intuitive idea of deterministic dependence between two quantities, one of which is viewed as primary and the other as secondary. A _____ then is a way to associate a unique output for each input of a specified type, for example, a real number or an element of a given set.
   a. Thing
   b. Function0
   c. Undefined
   d. Undefined

13. A _____ is a symbolic representation denoting a quantity or expression. It often represents an "unknown" quantity that has the potential to change.
   a. Variable0
   b. Thing
   c. Undefined
   d. Undefined

14. A pair of angles is _____ if their respective measures sum to 180 degrees.
   a. Supplementary0
   b. Concept
   c. Undefined
   d. Undefined

15. In mathematics, a _____ is a condition that a solution to an optimization problem must satisfy in order to be acceptable.
   a. Thing
   b. Constraint0
   c. Undefined
   d. Undefined

16. A _____ function is a function for which, intuitively, small changes in the input result in small changes in the output.
   a. Event
   b. Continuous0
   c. Undefined
   d. Undefined

17. The _____, the average in everyday English, which is also called the arithmetic _____ (and is distinguished from the geometric _____ or harmonic _____). The average is also called the sample _____. The expected value of a random variable, which is also called the population _____.
   a. Thing
   b. Mean0
   c. Undefined
   d. Undefined

18. A _____ is 360° or 2δ radians.
   a. Turn0
   b. Thing
   c. Undefined
   d. Undefined

19. _____ of a function of several variables is its derivative with respect to one of those variables with the others held constant as opposed to the total derivative, in which all variables are allowed to vary.
   a. Partial derivative0
   b. Thing
   c. Undefined
   d. Undefined

Chapter 3. Higher-Order Derivatives; Maxima and Minima

20. In mathematics, a _____ is a statement that can be proved on the basis of explicitly stated or previously agreed assumptions.
   a. Theorem0
   b. Thing
   c. Undefined
   d. Undefined

21. Two mathematical objects are equal if and only if they are precisely the same in every way. This defines a binary relation, _____, denoted by the sign of _____ "=" in such a way that the statement "x = y" means that x and y are equal.
   a. Equality0
   b. Thing
   c. Undefined
   d. Undefined

22. In physics and in _____ calculus, a spatial _____, or simply _____, is a concept characterized by a magnitude and a direction.
   a. Vector0
   b. Thing
   c. Undefined
   d. Undefined

23. An _____ is an equality that remains true regardless of the values of any variables that appear within it, to distinguish it from an equality which is true under more particular conditions.
   a. Identity0
   b. Thing
   c. Undefined
   d. Undefined

24. In mathematics, a _____ is a countable collection of open covers of a topological space that satisfies certain separation axioms.
   a. Development0
   b. Thing
   c. Undefined
   d. Undefined

25. Mathematical _____ is used to represent ideas.
   a. Notation0
   b. Thing
   c. Undefined
   d. Undefined

26. In physics, a _____ may refer to the scalar _____ or to the vector _____.
   a. Thing
   b. Potential0
   c. Undefined
   d. Undefined

27. In calculus, the _____ is a formula for the derivative of the composite of two functions.
   a. Concept
   b. Chain rule0
   c. Undefined
   d. Undefined

28. In mathematics, a _____ is the result of multiplying, or an expression that identifies factors to be multiplied.
   a. Thing
   b. Product0
   c. Undefined
   d. Undefined

29. The _____ governs the differentiation of products of differentiable functions.
   a. Product rule0
   b. Thing
   c. Undefined
   d. Undefined

Chapter 3. Higher-Order Derivatives; Maxima and Minima

30. _____ are objects, characters, or other concrete representations of ideas, concepts, or other abstractions.
    a. Symbols0
    b. Thing
    c. Undefined
    d. Undefined

31. A _____ is traditionally an infinitesimally small change in a variable.
    a. Differential0
    b. Thing
    c. Undefined
    d. Undefined

32. A _____ is a mathematical equation for an unknown function of one or several variables which relates the values of the function itself and of its derivatives of various orders.
    a. Differential equation0
    b. Thing
    c. Undefined
    d. Undefined

33. A _____ is one of the basic shapes of geometry: a polygon with three vertices and three sides which are straight line segments.
    a. Thing
    b. Triangle0
    c. Undefined
    d. Undefined

34. In Euclidean geometry, a _____ is the set of all points in a plane at a fixed distance, called the radius, from a given point, the center.
    a. Thing
    b. Circle0
    c. Undefined
    d. Undefined

35. _____ was an Italian physicist, mathematician, astronomer, and philosopher who is closely associated with the scientific revolution.
    a. Person
    b. Galileo Galilei0
    c. Undefined
    d. Undefined

36. Sir Isaac _____, was an English physicist, mathematician, astronomer, natural philosopher, and alchemist, regarded by many as the greatest figure in the history of science
    a. Person
    b. Newton0
    c. Undefined
    d. Undefined

37. Isaac Newton's _____ states the following:Every single point mass attracts every other point mass by a force pointing along the line combining the two.
    a. Law of gravitation0
    b. Thing
    c. Undefined
    d. Undefined

38. _____ are the cyclic rizing and falling of Earth's ocean surface caused by the tidal forces of the Moon and the sun acting on the oceans.
    a. Thing
    b. Tides0
    c. Undefined
    d. Undefined

39. _____ is a kind of property which exists as magnitude or multitude. It is among the basic classes of things along with quality, substance, change, and relation.

Chapter 3. Higher-Order Derivatives; Maxima and Minima

a. Thing
b. Amount0
c. Undefined
d. Undefined

40. _____ was a French mathematician and physicist who is best known for initiating the investigation of Fourier series and their application to problems of heat flow. The Fourier transform is also named in his honor.
   a. Joseph Fourier0
   b. Person
   c. Undefined
   d. Undefined

41. _____ is a physical property of a system that underlies the common notions of hot and cold; something that is hotter has the greater _____.
   a. Thing
   b. Temperature0
   c. Undefined
   d. Undefined

42. _____ is a set, with some particular properties and usually some additional structure, such as the operations of addition or multiplication, for instance.
   a. Space0
   b. Thing
   c. Undefined
   d. Undefined

43. _____ is the property of a physical object that quantifies the amount of matter and energy it is equivalent to.
   a. Mass0
   b. Thing
   c. Undefined
   d. Undefined

44. _____ is mass m per unit volume V.
   a. Density0
   b. Thing
   c. Undefined
   d. Undefined

45. In mathematics and the mathematical sciences, a _____ is a fixed, but possibly unspecified, value. This is in contrast to a variable, which is not fixed.
   a. Thing
   b. Constant0
   c. Undefined
   d. Undefined

46. A _____, or Ocean Surface Waves are surface waves that occur in the upper layer of the ocean.
   a. Water wave0
   b. Thing
   c. Undefined
   d. Undefined

47. _____, a field in mathematics, is the study of how functions change when their inputs change. The primary object of study in _____ is the derivative.
   a. Thing
   b. Differential calculus0
   c. Undefined
   d. Undefined

48. In acoustics and telecommunication, the _____ of a wave is a component frequency of the signal that is an integer multiple of the fundamental frequency.
   a. Harmonic0
   b. Thing
   c. Undefined
   d. Undefined

49. _____ is an adjective usually refering to being in the centre.

Chapter 3. Higher-Order Derivatives; Maxima and Minima

a. Central0
b. Thing
c. Undefined
d. Undefined

50. The word _____ comes from the Latin word linearis, which means created by lines.
a. Thing
b. Linear0
c. Undefined
d. Undefined

51. _____ is an approximation of a general function using a linear function more precisely, an affine function.
a. Thing
b. Linear approximation0
c. Undefined
d. Undefined

52. In mathematics, a _____ is a demonstration that, assuming certain axioms, some statement is necessarily true.
a. Thing
b. Proof0
c. Undefined
d. Undefined

53. _____ is a process of combining or accumulating. It may also refer to:
a. Thing
b. Integration0
c. Undefined
d. Undefined

54. In number theory, the _____ of arithmetic (or unique factorization theorem) states that every natural number greater than 1 can be written as a unique product of prime numbers.
a. Fundamental theorem0
b. Concept
c. Undefined
d. Undefined

55. _____ of calculus is the statement that the two central operations of calculus, differentiation and integration, are inverse operations: if a continuous function is first integrated and then differentiated, the original function is retrieved.
a. Fundamental Theorem of Calculus0
b. Thing
c. Undefined
d. Undefined

56. In common philosophical language, a proposition or _____, is the content of an assertion, that is, it is true-or-false and defined by the meaning of a particular piece of language.
a. Concept
b. Statement0
c. Undefined
d. Undefined

57. A _____ is the result of the addition of a set of numbers. The numbers may be natural numbers, complex numbers, matrices, or still more complicated objects. An infinite _____ is a subtle procedure known as a series.
a. Thing
b. Sum0
c. Undefined
d. Undefined

58. In mathematics, a _____ is a rectangular table of numbers or, more generally, a table consisting of abstract quantities that can be added and multiplied.
a. Thing
b. Matrix0
c. Undefined
d. Undefined

59. A _____ is the part of the dividend that is left over when the dividend is not evenly divisible by the divisor.

a. Remainder0
b. Thing
c. Undefined
d. Undefined

60. In mathematics, the _____(e) for L-functions are a class of summation formulae, expressing sums taken over the complex number zeroes of a given L-function, typically in terms of quantities studied by number theory by use of the theory of special functions.
   a. Explicit formula0
   b. Thing
   c. Undefined
   d. Undefined

61. In mathematics, science including computer science, linguistics and engineering, an _____ is, generally speaking, an independent variable or input to a function.
   a. Thing
   b. Argument0
   c. Undefined
   d. Undefined

62. The _____ of a function is an extension of the concept of a sum, and are identified or found through the use of integration.
   a. Integral0
   b. Thing
   c. Undefined
   d. Undefined

63. A _____ is the sum of the elements of a sequence.
   a. Series0
   b. Thing
   c. Undefined
   d. Undefined

64. _____ is the state of being greater than any finite real or natural number, however large.
   a. Infinite0
   b. Thing
   c. Undefined
   d. Undefined

65. In mathematics, the _____ is a representation of a function as an infinite sum of terms calculated from the values of its derivatives at a single point.
   a. Thing
   b. Taylor series0
   c. Undefined
   d. Undefined

66. _____ has many meanings, most of which simply .
   a. Power0
   b. Thing
   c. Undefined
   d. Undefined

67. _____ in one variable is an infinite series of the form
   a. Power series0
   b. Thing
   c. Undefined
   d. Undefined

68. An _____ is a combination of numbers, operators, grouping symbols and/or free variables and bound variables arranged in a meaningful way which can be evaluated..
   a. Expression0
   b. Thing
   c. Undefined
   d. Undefined

Chapter 3. Higher-Order Derivatives; Maxima and Minima

69. in mathematics, maxima and minima, known collectively as _____, are the largest value maximum or smallest value minimum, that a function takes in a point either within a given neighborhood or on the function domain in its entirety global extremum.
    a. Extrema0
    b. Thing
    c. Undefined
    d. Undefined

70. Kepler's laws of _____ are his primary contributions to astronomy/astrophysics. Kepler, a German mathematician, studied the observations of the legendarily precise Danish astronomer Tycho Brahe, and found around 1605 that these observations followed three relatively simple mathematical laws.
    a. Thing
    b. Planetary motion0
    c. Undefined
    d. Undefined

71. A _____ signifies a point or points of probability on a subject e.g., the _____ of creativity, which allows for the formation of rule or norm or law by interpretation of the phenomena events that can be created.
    a. Thing
    b. Principle0
    c. Undefined
    d. Undefined

72. The _____ of a solid object is the three-dimensional concept of how much space it occupies, often quantified numerically.
    a. Volume0
    b. Thing
    c. Undefined
    d. Undefined

73. In mathematics, a _____ is the set of all points in three-dimensional space (R^3) which are at distance r from a fixed point of that space, where r is a positive real number called the radius of the _____. The fixed point is called the center or centre, and is not part of the _____ itself.
    a. Thing
    b. Sphere0
    c. Undefined
    d. Undefined

74. _____ was a German mathematician and philosopher. He invented calculus independently of Newton, and his notation is the one in general use since.
    a. Leibniz0
    b. Person
    c. Undefined
    d. Undefined

75. _____ is the transport of people on a trip/journey or the process or time involved in a person or object moving from one location to another.
    a. Thing
    b. Travel0
    c. Undefined
    d. Undefined

76. A _____ is a unit of length in the metric system, equal to one thousand metres, the current SI base unit of length
    a. Kilometer0
    b. Thing
    c. Undefined
    d. Undefined

77. _____ of an object is its speed in a particular direction.
    a. Thing
    b. Velocity0
    c. Undefined
    d. Undefined

Chapter 3. Higher-Order Derivatives; Maxima and Minima

78. In mathematics, the word _____ is used informally to refer to certain distinct bodies of knowledge about mathematics.
   a. Theoretical0
   b. Thing
   c. Undefined
   d. Undefined

79. In probability theory, _____ are various sets of outcomes (a subset of the sample space) to which a probability is assigned.
   a. Events0
   b. Thing
   c. Undefined
   d. Undefined

80. _____, Greek for "knowledge of nature," is the branch of science concerned with the discovery and characterization of universal laws which govern matter, energy, space, and time.
   a. Physics0
   b. Thing
   c. Undefined
   d. Undefined

81. In mathematics, the _____ f is the collection of all ordered pairs . In particular, graph means the graphical representation of this collection, in the form of a curve or surface, together with axes, etc. Graphing on a Cartesian plane is sometimes referred to as curve sketching.
   a. Graph of a function0
   b. Thing
   c. Undefined
   d. Undefined

82. An _____ or an extremal point is a point that belongs to the extremity of something.
   a. Extreme point0
   b. Thing
   c. Undefined
   d. Undefined

83. In geographic information systems, a _____ comprises an entity with a geographic location, typically determined by points, arcs, or polygons. Carriageways and cadastres exemplify _____ data.
   a. Feature0
   b. Thing
   c. Undefined
   d. Undefined

84. In linear algebra, real numbers are called scalars and relate to vectors in a vector space through the operation of _____ multiplication, in which a vector can be multiplied by a number to produce another vector.
   a. Thing
   b. Scalar0
   c. Undefined
   d. Undefined

85. In mathematics, maxima and minima, known collectively as extrema, are the largest value maximum or smallest value minimum, that a function takes in a point either within a given neighborhood local _____ or on the function domain in its entirety global _____.
   a. Extremum0
   b. Thing
   c. Undefined
   d. Undefined

86. _____ is a point on the domain of a function
   a. Critical point0
   b. Thing
   c. Undefined
   d. Undefined

87. _____ determines whether a given critical point of a function is a maximum, a minimum, or neither.

Chapter 3. Higher-Order Derivatives; Maxima and Minima

    a. Thing
    b. First Derivative Test0
    c. Undefined
    d. Undefined

88. In the most general terms, a _____ for a smooth function (curve, surface or hypersurface) is a point such that the curve/surface/etc. in the neighborhood of this point lies on different sides of the tangent at this point. In certain contexts the definition may vary. It is most frequently used at critical points.
    a. Thing
    b. Saddle point0
    c. Undefined
    d. Undefined

89. In vector calculus, the _____ of a scalar field is a vector field which points in the direction of the greatest rate of increase of the scalar field, and whose magnitude is the greatest rate of change.
    a. Gradient0
    b. Thing
    c. Undefined
    d. Undefined

90. In mathematics, in the field of group theory, a _____ of a group is a quasisimple subnormal subgroup.
    a. Concept
    b. Component0
    c. Undefined
    d. Undefined

91. The _____ is the lowest point in a certain portion of a graph.
    a. Relative minimum0
    b. Thing
    c. Undefined
    d. Undefined

92. In mathematics, the _____ of a coordinate system is the point where the axes of the system intersect.
    a. Thing
    b. Origin0
    c. Undefined
    d. Undefined

93. In mathematics, an _____ is a statement about the relative size or order of two objects.
    a. Thing
    b. Inequality0
    c. Undefined
    d. Undefined

94. The _____ is the highest point in a certain portion of a graph.
    a. Thing
    b. Relative maximum0
    c. Undefined
    d. Undefined

95. _____ traditionally refers to the statistical process of determining comparable scores on different forms of an exam
    a. Equating0
    b. Thing
    c. Undefined
    d. Undefined

96. A _____ is a polynomial function of the form $f(x) = ax^2 + bx + c$, where a, b, c are real numbers and a , 0.
    a. Quadratic function0
    b. Event
    c. Undefined
    d. Undefined

97. In mathematics, _____ is an elementary arithmetic operation. When one of the numbers is a whole number, _____ is the repeated sum of the other number.

Chapter 3. Higher-Order Derivatives; Maxima and Minima

a. Multiplication0   b. Thing
c. Undefined   d. Undefined

98. In statistics, a _____ measure is one which is measuring what is supposed to measure.
a. Valid0   b. Thing
c. Undefined   d. Undefined

99. A _____ is a function for which, intuitively, small changes in the input result in small changes in the output.
a. Continuous function0   b. Event
c. Undefined   d. Undefined

100. In linear algebra, a _____ is a square matrix, A, that is equal to its transpose.
a. Thing   b. Symmetric Matrix0
c. Undefined   d. Undefined

101. In elementary algebra, an _____ is a set that contains every real number between two indicated numbers and may contain the two numbers themselves.
a. Thing   b. Interval0
c. Undefined   d. Undefined

102. In plane geometry, a _____ is a polygon with four equal sides, four right angles, and parallel opposite sides. In algebra, the _____ of a number is that number multiplied by itself.
a. Thing   b. Square0
c. Undefined   d. Undefined

103. _____ is a concept that permeates much of inferential statistics and descriptive statistics. More properly, it is "the sum of the squared deviations".
a. Sum of squares0   b. Thing
c. Undefined   d. Undefined

104. A vector can be thought of as an arrow. It has a length, called its magnitude, and it points in some particular direction. A linear transformation inputs a vector and changes it, usually changing both its magnitude and its direction. An eigenvector of a given linear transformation is a vector which is simply multiplied by a constant called the _____ during that transformation.
a. Eigenvalue0   b. Thing
c. Undefined   d. Undefined

105. _____ is a branch of mathematics concerning the study of structure, relation and quantity.
a. Algebra0   b. Concept
c. Undefined   d. Undefined

106. A _____ consists of one quarter of the coordinate plane.
a. Thing   b. Quadrant0
c. Undefined   d. Undefined

107. An _____ is a straight line around which a geometric figure can be rotated.

Chapter 3. Higher-Order Derivatives; Maxima and Minima

a. Thing
c. Undefined
b. Axis0
d. Undefined

108. In mathematical analysis and related areas of mathematics, a set is called _____, if it is, in a certain sense, of finite size.
a. Thing
c. Undefined
b. Bounded0
d. Undefined

109. In mathematics, an _____ is a theorem with a statement beginning 'there exist ...'. That is, in more formal terms of symbolic logic, it is a theorem with a statement involving the existential quantifier.
a. Thing
c. Undefined
b. Existence theorem0
d. Undefined

110. In mathematics, a _____ is a connected curve that does not intersect itself and ends at the same point in which it starts.
a. Thing
c. Undefined
b. Closed curve0
d. Undefined

111. In mathematics, the concept of a _____ tries to capture the intuitive idea of a geometrical one-dimensional and continuous object. A simple example is the circle.
a. Curve0
c. Undefined
b. Thing
d. Undefined

112. In mathematics, _____ is a part of the set theoretic notion of function.
a. Image0
c. Undefined
b. Thing
d. Undefined

113. In mathematics, _____ are the intuitive idea of a geometrical one-dimensional and continuous object.
a. Curves0
c. Undefined
b. Thing
d. Undefined

114. _____ is a trigonemtric function that is important when studying triangles and modeling periodic phenomena, among other applications.
a. Sine0
c. Undefined
b. Thing
d. Undefined

115. In mathematics, a _____ is a two-dimensional manifold or surface that is perfectly flat.
a. Thing
c. Undefined
b. Plane0
d. Undefined

116. A _____ is a three-dimensional solid object bounded by six square faces, facets, or sides, with three meeting at each vertex.
a. Thing
c. Undefined
b. Cube0
d. Undefined

117. In geometry, a _____ is a three-dimensional figure formed by six parallelograms.

Chapter 3. Higher-Order Derivatives; Maxima and Minima

a. Parallelepiped0
b. Thing
c. Undefined
d. Undefined

118. In mathematics, an inequality is a statement about the relative size or order of two objects. For example 14 > 10, or 14 is _____ 10.
   a. Greater than0
   b. Thing
   c. Undefined
   d. Undefined

119. _____ was an Italian mathematician, whose work was of exceptional philosophical value. The author of over 200 books and papers, he was a founder of mathematical logic and set theory, to which he contributed much notation. The standard axiomatization of the natural numbers is named in his honor. He spent most of his career teaching mathematics at the University of Turin.
   a. Person
   b. Giuseppe Peano0
   c. Undefined
   d. Undefined

120. In mathematics, a _____ is a quadric surface, with the following equation in Cartesian coordinates: $(x/_a)^2 + (y/_b)^2 = 1$.
   a. Cylinder0
   b. Thing
   c. Undefined
   d. Undefined

121. In geometry, a _____ is defined as a quadrilateral where all four of its angles are right angles.
   a. Rectangle0
   b. Thing
   c. Undefined
   d. Undefined

122. _____ are a method for finding the extrema of a function of several variables subject to one or more constraints: it is the basic tool in nonlinear constrained optimization.
   a. Lagrange multipliers0
   b. Thing
   c. Undefined
   d. Undefined

123. In mathematics, a _____ may be described informally as a number that can be given by an infinite decimal representation.
   a. Real number0
   b. Thing
   c. Undefined
   d. Undefined

124. In trigonometry, the _____ is a function defined as $\tan x = {}^{\sin x}/_{\cos x}$. The function is so-named because it can be defined as the length of a certain segment of a _____ (in the geometric sense) to the unit circle. In plane geometry, a line is _____ to a curve, at some point, if both line and curve pass through the point with the same direction.
   a. Thing
   b. Tangent0
   c. Undefined
   d. Undefined

125. In mathematics, _____ is synonymous with perpendicular when used as a simple adjective that is not part of any longer phrase with a standard definition. It means at right angles. It comes from the Greek á½€Ï Î¸ÏŒÏ, orthos, meaning "straight", used by Euclid to mean right; and Î³Ï‰Î½Î¯Î± gonia, meaning angle. Two streets that cross each other at a right angle are _____ to one another.

Chapter 3. Higher-Order Derivatives; Maxima and Minima

a. Orthogonal0
b. Thing
c. Undefined
d. Undefined

126. In geometry, two lines or planes if one falls on the other in such a way as to create congruent adjacent angles. The term may be used as a noun or adjective. Thus, referring to Figure 1, the line AB is the _____ to CD through the point B.
a. Thing
b. Perpendicular0
c. Undefined
d. Undefined

127. A _____ of a number is the product of that number with any integer.
a. Multiple0
b. Thing
c. Undefined
d. Undefined

128. In a mathematical proof or a syllogism, a _____ is a statement that is the logical consequence of preceding statements.
a. Concept
b. Conclusion0
c. Undefined
d. Undefined

129. A _____ is a mathematical statement which follows easily from a previously proven statement, typically a mathematical theorem.
a. Thing
b. Corollary0
c. Undefined
d. Undefined

130. In mathematics, two quantities are called _____ if they vary in such a way that one of the quantities is a constant multiple of the other, or equivalently if they have a constant ratio.
a. Thing
b. Proportional0
c. Undefined
d. Undefined

131. _____ is the property of two events happening at the same time in at least one reference frame.
a. Simultaneous0
b. Thing
c. Undefined
d. Undefined

132. _____ are a set of equations containing multiple variables.
a. Systems of equations0
b. Thing
c. Undefined
d. Undefined

133. In classical geometry, a _____ of a circle or sphere is any line segment from its center to its boundary. By extension, the _____ of a circle or sphere is the length of any such segment. The _____ is half the diameter. In science and engineering the term _____ of curvature is commonly used as a synonym for _____.
a. Radius0
b. Thing
c. Undefined
d. Undefined

134. The metre (or _____, see spelling differences) is a measure of length. It is the basic unit of length in the metric system and in the International System of Units (SI), used around the world for general and scientific purposes.
a. Meter0
b. Concept
c. Undefined
d. Undefined

Chapter 3. Higher-Order Derivatives; Maxima and Minima

135. The _____ is the distance around a closed curve. _____ is a kind of perimeter.
a. Thing
b. Circumference0
c. Undefined
d. Undefined

136. _____ are any documents that aim to streamline particular processes according to a set routine.
a. Thing
b. Guidelines0
c. Undefined
d. Undefined

137. In combinatorial mathematics, a _____ is an un-ordered collection of unique elements.
a. Concept
b. Combination0
c. Undefined
d. Undefined

138. A _____ consists either of a suggested explanation for a phenomenon or of a reasoned proposal suggesting a possible correlation between multiple phenomena.
a. Thing
b. Hypothesis0
c. Undefined
d. Undefined

139. In mathematics, an _____ .
a. Thing
b. Ellipse0
c. Undefined
d. Undefined

140. In mathematics, a _____ is a constant multiplicative factor of a certain object. The object can be such things as a variable, a vector, a function, etc. For example, the _____ of $9x^2$ is 9.
a. Coefficient0
b. Thing
c. Undefined
d. Undefined

141. _____ element of an element x with respect to a binary operation * with identity element e is an element y such that x * y = y * x = e. In particular,
a. Thing
b. Inverse0
c. Undefined
d. Undefined

142. In algebra, a _____ is a function depending on n that associates a scalar, det(A), to every $n \times n$ square matrix A.
a. Thing
b. Determinant0
c. Undefined
d. Undefined

143. An _____ is when two lines intersect somewhere on a plane creating a right angle at intersection
a. Axes0
b. Thing
c. Undefined
d. Undefined

144. _____ represents the combinations of goods and services that a consumer can purchase given current prices and his income.
a. Thing
b. Budget constraint0
c. Undefined
d. Undefined

145. In economics, an _____ is a contour line drawn through the set of points at which the same quantity of output is produced while changing the quantities of two or more inputs.

Chapter 3. Higher-Order Derivatives; Maxima and Minima

a. Isoquant0
b. Thing
c. Undefined
d. Undefined

146. In mathematics, a _____ of a k-place relation $L \subseteq X_1 \times \ldots \times X_k$ is one of the sets X_j, $1 \leq j \leq k$. In the special case where k = 2 and $L \subseteq X_1 \times X_2$ is a function $L : X_1 \to X_2$, it is conventional to refer to X_1 as the _____ of the function and to refer to X_2 as the codomain of the function.
a. Domain0
b. Thing
c. Undefined
d. Undefined

147. _____ determines whether a given stationary point of a function is a maximum or a minimum.
a. Second derivative test0
b. Thing
c. Undefined
d. Undefined

148. A _____ can refer to a line joining two nonadjacent vertices of a polygon or polyhedron, or in some contexts any upward or downward sloping line. .
a. Thing
b. Diagonal0
c. Undefined
d. Undefined

149. In astronomy, geography, geometry and related sciences and contexts, a plane is said to be _____ at a given point if it is locally perpendicular to the gradient of the gravity field, i.e., with the direction of the gravitational force at that point.
a. Thing
b. Horizontal0
c. Undefined
d. Undefined

150. In geometry, a _____ is the intersection of a body in 2-dimensional space with a line, or of a body in 3-dimensional space with a plane
a. Thing
b. Cross section0
c. Undefined
d. Undefined

151. _____ is the distance around a given two-dimensional object. As a general rule, the _____ of a polygon can always be calculated by adding all the length of the sides together. So, the formula for triangles is P = a + b + c, where a, b and c stand for each side of it. For quadrilaterals the equation is P = a + b + c + d. For equilateral polygons, P = na, where n is the number of sides and a is the side length.
a. Thing
b. Perimeter0
c. Undefined
d. Undefined

152. A _____ given two distinct points A and B on the _____, is the set of points C on the line containing points A and B such that A is not strictly between C and B.
a. Ray0
b. Thing
c. Undefined
d. Undefined

153. _____ is electromagnetic radiation with a wavelength that is visible to the eye (visible _____) or, in a technical or scientific context, electromagnetic radiation of any wavelength.
a. Light0
b. Thing
c. Undefined
d. Undefined

Chapter 3. Higher-Order Derivatives; Maxima and Minima

154. _____ asserts that the maximum output of a technologically-determined production process is a mathematical function of input factors of production.
 a. Thing
 b. Production function0
 c. Undefined
 d. Undefined

155. In mathematics, an _____ is a generalization for the concept of a function in which the dependent variable may not be given explicitly in terms of the independent variable.
 a. Implicit function0
 b. Thing
 c. Undefined
 d. Undefined

156. A _____ is a set of numbers that designate location in a given reference system, such as x,y in a planar _____ system or an x,y,z in a three-dimensional _____ system.
 a. Coordinate0
 b. Thing
 c. Undefined
 d. Undefined

157. In functional analysis and related areas of mathematics the _____ set of a given subset of a vector space is a certain set in the dual space.
 a. Polar0
 b. Thing
 c. Undefined
 d. Undefined

158. _____ means of or relating to the French philosopher and mathematician René Descartes.
 a. Thing
 b. Cartesian0
 c. Undefined
 d. Undefined

159. _____ is often used to describe the measurement of the steepness, incline, gradient, or grade of a straight line. The _____ is defined as the ratio of the "rise" divided by the "run" between two points on a line, or in other words, the ratio of the altitude change to the horizontal distance between any two points on the line.
 a. Thing
 b. Slope0
 c. Undefined
 d. Undefined

160. An _____ is a function which does the reverse of a given function.
 a. Inverse function0
 b. Thing
 c. Undefined
 d. Undefined

161. Equivalence is the condition of being _____ or essentially equal.
 a. Thing
 b. Equivalent0
 c. Undefined
 d. Undefined

162. In mathematics, _____ are two-dimensional manifolds or surfaces that are perfectly flat.
 a. Planes0
 b. Thing
 c. Undefined
 d. Undefined

163. In set theory and other branches of mathematics, two kinds of complements are defined, the relative _____ and the absolute _____.

Chapter 3. Higher-Order Derivatives; Maxima and Minima

a. Complement0
b. Thing
c. Undefined
d. Undefined

164. Mathematical _____ are demonstrations that, assuming certain axioms, some statement is necessarily true.
   a. Thing
   b. Proofs0
   c. Undefined
   d. Undefined

165. _____ is to give an equation R(x,y) = S(x,y) that at least in part has the same graph as y = f(x).
   a. Implicit differentiation0
   b. Thing
   c. Undefined
   d. Undefined

166. A _____ is a negotiable instrument instructing a financial institution to pay a specific amount of a specific currency from a specific demand account held in the maker/depositor's name with that institution. Both the maker and payee may be natural persons or legal entities.
   a. Thing
   b. Check0
   c. Undefined
   d. Undefined

167. In mathematics, a _____ is a collection of points which share a property.
   a. Thing
   b. Locus0
   c. Undefined
   d. Undefined

168. In mathematics, _____ is the decomposition of an object into a product of other objects, or factors, which when multiplied together give the original.
   a. Factoring0
   b. Thing
   c. Undefined
   d. Undefined

169. In mathematics, factorization (British English: factorisation) or factoring is the decomposition of an object (for example, a number, a polynomial, or a matrix) into a product of other objects, or _____, which when multiplied together give the original.
   a. Thing
   b. Factors0
   c. Undefined
   d. Undefined

170. In mathematics, a _____ is an expression that is constructed from one or more variables and constants, using only the operations of addition, subtraction, multiplication, and constant positive whole number exponents. is a _____. Note in particular that division by an expression containing a variable is not in general allowed in polynomials. [1]
   a. Polynomial0
   b. Thing
   c. Undefined
   d. Undefined

171. In mathematics, a _____ of a complex-valued function f is a member x of the domain of f such that f(x) vanishes at x, that is, x : f (x) = 0.
   a. Root0
   b. Thing
   c. Undefined
   d. Undefined

172. In mathematics, the _____ is a conic section generated by the intersection of a right circular conical surface and a plane parallel to a generating straight line of that surface. It can also be defined as locus of points in a plane which are equidistant from a given point.

Chapter 3. Higher-Order Derivatives; Maxima and Minima

a. Parabola0
b. Thing
c. Undefined
d. Undefined

173. In mathematics, the _____ of two sets A and B is the set that contains all elements of A that also belong to B (or equivalently, all elements of B that also belong to A), but no other elements.
  a. Intersection0
  b. Thing
  c. Undefined
  d. Undefined

174. An _____ is a type of quadric surface that is a higher dimensional analogue of an ellipse.
  a. Ellipsoid0
  b. Thing
  c. Undefined
  d. Undefined

175. The _____ is a surface that belongs to the class of saddle surfaces and its name derives from the observation that a saddle for a monkey requires three depressions: two for the legs, and one for the tail.
  a. Thing
  b. Monkey saddle0
  c. Undefined
  d. Undefined

176. In mathematics, a _____ case is a limiting case in which a class of object changes its nature so as to belong to another, usually simpler, class.
  a. Degenerate0
  b. Thing
  c. Undefined
  d. Undefined

177. In economics, economic _____ is simply a state of the world where economic forces are balanced and in the absence of external influences the values of economic variables will not change.
  a. Equilibrium0
  b. Thing
  c. Undefined
  d. Undefined

178. In mathematics, a _____ is a homogeneous polynomial of degree two in a number of variables.
  a. Quadratic form0
  b. Thing
  c. Undefined
  d. Undefined

179. _____ is a synonym for information.
  a. Data0
  b. Thing
  c. Undefined
  d. Undefined

180. In regression analysis, _____, also known as ordinary _____ analysis is a method for linear regression that determines the values of unknown quantities in a statistical model by minimizing the sum of the residuals difference between the predicted and observed values squared.
  a. Least squares0
  b. Thing
  c. Undefined
  d. Undefined

181. _____ is a measure of difference for interval and ratio variables between the observed value and the mean.
  a. Deviation0
  b. Thing
  c. Undefined
  d. Undefined

Chapter 4. Vector-Valued Functions

1. In physics and in _____ calculus, a spatial _____, or simply _____, is a concept characterized by a magnitude and a direction.
   a. Vector0
   b. Thing
   c. Undefined
   d. Undefined

2. _____ are the cyclic rizing and falling of Earth's ocean surface caused by the tidal forces of the Moon and the sun acting on the oceans.
   a. Thing
   b. Tides0
   c. Undefined
   d. Undefined

3. A _____, as defined by the International Astronomical Union, is a celestial body orbiting a star or stellar remnant that is massive enough to be rounded by its own gravity, not massive enough to cause thermonuclear fusion in its core, and has cleared its neighboring region of planetesimals.
   a. Thing
   b. Planet0
   c. Undefined
   d. Undefined

4. The mathematical concept of a _____ expresses the intuitive idea of deterministic dependence between two quantities, one of which is viewed as primary and the other as secondary. A _____ then is a way to associate a unique output for each input of a specified type, for example, a real number or an element of a given set.
   a. Thing
   b. Function0
   c. Undefined
   d. Undefined

5. _____ is a construction in vector calculus which associates a vector to every point in a locally Euclidean space.
   a. Vector field0
   b. Thing
   c. Undefined
   d. Undefined

6. In vector calculus, the _____ of a scalar field is a vector field which points in the direction of the greatest rate of increase of the scalar field, and whose magnitude is the greatest rate of change.
   a. Thing
   b. Gradient0
   c. Undefined
   d. Undefined

7. _____ is a mathematical subject that includes the study of limits, derivatives, integrals, and power series and constitutes a major part of modern university curriculum.
   a. Thing
   b. Calculus0
   c. Undefined
   d. Undefined

8. A _____ is traditionally an infinitesimally small change in a variable.
   a. Differential0
   b. Thing
   c. Undefined
   d. Undefined

9. _____, a field in mathematics, is the study of how functions change when their inputs change. The primary object of study in _____ is the derivative.
   a. Thing
   b. Differential calculus0
   c. Undefined
   d. Undefined

10. _____ is an operator that measures the magnitude of a vector field's source or sink at a given point; the _____ of a vector field is a signed scalar.

Chapter 4. Vector-Valued Functions

a. Thing
b. Divergence0
c. Undefined
d. Undefined

11. Sir Isaac _____, was an English physicist, mathematician, astronomer, natural philosopher, and alchemist, regarded by many as the greatest figure in the history of science
    a. Person
    b. Newton0
    c. Undefined
    d. Undefined

12. In trigonometry, the _____ is a function defined as $\tan x = \sin x / \cos x$. The function is so-named because it can be defined as the length of a certain segment of a _____ (in the geometric sense) to the unit circle. In plane geometry, a line is _____ to a curve, at some point, if both line and curve pass through the point with the same direction.
    a. Thing
    b. Tangent0
    c. Undefined
    d. Undefined

13. _____ has two distinct but etymologically-related meanings: one in geometry and one in trigonometry.
    a. Thing
    b. Tangent line0
    c. Undefined
    d. Undefined

14. In mathematics, the concept of a _____ tries to capture the intuitive idea of a geometrical one-dimensional and continuous object. A simple example is the circle.
    a. Curve0
    b. Thing
    c. Undefined
    d. Undefined

15. In mathematics, _____ are the intuitive idea of a geometrical one-dimensional and continuous object.
    a. Thing
    b. Curves0
    c. Undefined
    d. Undefined

16. In mathematics, _____ is a part of the set theoretic notion of function.
    a. Thing
    b. Image0
    c. Undefined
    d. Undefined

17. The _____ of a function is an extension of the concept of a sum, and are identified or found through the use of integration.
    a. Integral0
    b. Thing
    c. Undefined
    d. Undefined

18. _____ is defined as the rate of change or derivative with respect to time of velocity.
    a. Thing
    b. Acceleration0
    c. Undefined
    d. Undefined

19. In mathematics, _____ is an elementary arithmetic operation. When one of the numbers is a whole number, _____ is the repeated sum of the other number.
    a. Thing
    b. Multiplication0
    c. Undefined
    d. Undefined

20. In mathematics, a _____ is the result of multiplying, or an expression that identifies factors to be multiplied.

Chapter 4. Vector-Valued Functions

a. Thing
b. Product0
c. Undefined
d. Undefined

21. The _____ governs the differentiation of products of differentiable functions.
a. Thing
b. Product rule0
c. Undefined
d. Undefined

22. In calculus, the _____ is a formula for the derivative of the composite of two functions.
a. Concept
b. Chain rule0
c. Undefined
d. Undefined

23. _____ is a binary operation on two vectors in a three-dimensional Euclidean space that results in another vector which is perpedicular to the two input vectors.
a. Cross product0
b. Thing
c. Undefined
d. Undefined

24. A _____ is the result of the addition of a set of numbers. The numbers may be natural numbers, complex numbers, matrices, or still more complicated objects. An infinite _____ is a subtle procedure known as a series.
a. Thing
b. Sum0
c. Undefined
d. Undefined

25. In calculus, the _____ in differentiation is a method of finding the derivative of a function that is the sum of two other functions for which derivatives exist.
a. Thing
b. Sum Rule0
c. Undefined
d. Undefined

26. In linear algebra, real numbers are called scalars and relate to vectors in a vector space through the operation of _____ multiplication, in which a vector can be multiplied by a number to produce another vector.
a. Scalar0
b. Thing
c. Undefined
d. Undefined

27. _____ is one of the basic operations defining a vector space in linear algebra.
a. Thing
b. Scalar multiplication0
c. Undefined
d. Undefined

28. In mathematics, in the field of group theory, a _____ of a group is a quasisimple subnormal subgroup.
a. Concept
b. Component0
c. Undefined
d. Undefined

29. The _____ is a measurement of how a function changes when the values of its inputs change.
a. Thing
b. Derivative0
c. Undefined
d. Undefined

30. In mathematics, the _____, also known as the scalar product, is a binary operation which takes two vectors over the real numbers R and returns a real-valued scalar quantity. It is the standard inner product of the Euclidean space.

a. Thing
b. Dot product0
c. Undefined
d. Undefined

31. In geometry, two lines or planes if one falls on the other in such a way as to create congruent adjacent angles. The term may be used as a noun or adjective. Thus, referring to Figure 1, the line AB is the _____ to CD through the point B.
   a. Thing
   b. Perpendicular0
   c. Undefined
   d. Undefined

32. In mathematics and the mathematical sciences, a _____ is a fixed, but possibly unspecified, value. This is in contrast to a variable, which is not fixed.
   a. Thing
   b. Constant0
   c. Undefined
   d. Undefined

33. _____ of an object is its speed in a particular direction.
   a. Velocity0
   b. Thing
   c. Undefined
   d. Undefined

34. In plane geometry, a _____ is a polygon with four equal sides, four right angles, and parallel opposite sides. In algebra, the _____ of a number is that number multiplied by itself.
   a. Thing
   b. Square0
   c. Undefined
   d. Undefined

35. _____ is often used to describe the measurement of the steepness, incline, gradient, or grade of a straight line. The _____ is defined as the ratio of the "rise" divided by the "run" between two points on a line, or in other words, the ratio of the altitude change to the horizontal distance between any two points on the line.
   a. Slope0
   b. Thing
   c. Undefined
   d. Undefined

36. The word _____ comes from the Latin word linearis, which means created by lines.
   a. Thing
   b. Linear0
   c. Undefined
   d. Undefined

37. A _____ is a first degree polynomial mathematical function of the form: f(x) = mx + b where m and b are real constants and x is a real variable.
   a. Linear function0
   b. Thing
   c. Undefined
   d. Undefined

38. _____ is a function whose values do not vary and thus are constant.
   a. Thing
   b. Constant function0
   c. Undefined
   d. Undefined

39. Initial objects are also called _____, and terminal objects are also called final.
   a. Coterminal0
   b. Thing
   c. Undefined
   d. Undefined

Chapter 4. Vector-Valued Functions

40. In mathematics, the _____ is a conic section generated by the intersection of a right circular conical surface and a plane parallel to a generating straight line of that surface. It can also be defined as locus of points in a plane which are equidistant from a given point.
    a. Parabola0
    b. Thing
    c. Undefined
    d. Undefined

41. In mathematics, a _____ is a two-dimensional manifold or surface that is perfectly flat.
    a. Thing
    b. Plane0
    c. Undefined
    d. Undefined

42. In mathematics, a _____ function in the sense of algebraic geometry is an everywhere-defined, polynomial function on an algebraic variety V with values in the field K over which V is defined.
    a. Regular0
    b. Thing
    c. Undefined
    d. Undefined

43. _____ is a trigonemtric function that is important when studying triangles and modeling periodic phenomena, among other applications.
    a. Thing
    b. Sine0
    c. Undefined
    d. Undefined

44. In physics, _____ is an influence that may cause an object to accelerate. It may be experienced as a lift, a push, or a pull. The actual acceleration of the body is determined by the vector sum of all forces acting on it, known as net _____ or resultant _____.
    a. Thing
    b. Force0
    c. Undefined
    d. Undefined

45. _____ is the property of a physical object that quantifies the amount of matter and energy it is equivalent to.
    a. Mass0
    b. Thing
    c. Undefined
    d. Undefined

46. _____ is the design, analysis, and/or construction of works for practical purposes.
    a. Engineering0
    b. Thing
    c. Undefined
    d. Undefined

47. In mathematics, the _____ of a coordinate system is the point where the axes of the system Intersect.
    a. Origin0
    b. Thing
    c. Undefined
    d. Undefined

48. _____ the expected value of a random variable displays the average or central value of the variable. It is a summary value of the distribution of the variable.
    a. Thing
    b. Determining0
    c. Undefined
    d. Undefined

49. A _____ is a mathematical equation for an unknown function of one or several variables which relates the values of the function itself and of its derivatives of various orders.

Chapter 4. Vector-Valued Functions

    a. Thing
    c. Undefined
    b. Differential equation0
    d. Undefined

50. In Euclidean geometry, a _____ is the set of all points in a plane at a fixed distance, called the radius, from a given point, the center.
    a. Thing
    c. Undefined
    b. Circle0
    d. Undefined

51. In classical geometry, a _____ of a circle or sphere is any line segment from its center to its boundary. By extension, the _____ of a circle or sphere is the length of any such segment. The _____ is half the diameter. In science and engineering the term _____ of curvature is commonly used as a synonym for _____.
    a. Radius0
    c. Undefined
    b. Thing
    d. Undefined

52. In geometry, the _____ of an object is a point in some sense in the middle of the object.
    a. Center0
    c. Undefined
    b. Thing
    d. Undefined

53. In mathematics, the additive inverse, or _____ of a number n is the number that, when added to n, yields zero. The additive inverse of n is denoted −n. For example, 7 is −7, because 7 + (−7) = 0, and the additive inverse of −0.3 is 0.3, because −0.3 + 0.3 = 0.
    a. Thing
    c. Undefined
    b. Opposite0
    d. Undefined

54. In statistics the _____ of an event i is the number n_i of times the event occurred in the experiment or the study. These frequencies are often graphically represented in histograms.
    a. Concept
    c. Undefined
    b. Frequency0
    d. Undefined

55. In mathematics, the _____ of a number n is the number that, when added to n, yields zero. The _____ of n is denoted −n. For example, 7 is −7, because 7 + (−7) = 0, and the _____ of −0.3 is 0.3, because −0.3 + 0.3 = 0.
    a. Thing
    c. Undefined
    b. Additive inverse0
    d. Undefined

56. A _____ is a special kind of ratio, indicating a relationship between two measurements with different units, such as miles to gallons or cents to pounds.
    a. Rate0
    c. Undefined
    b. Thing
    d. Undefined

57. In physics, an _____ is the path that an object makes around another object while under the influence of a source of centripetal force, such as gravity.
    a. Thing
    c. Undefined
    b. Orbit0
    d. Undefined

58. In business, particularly accounting, a _____ is the time intervals that the accounts, statement, payments, or other calculations cover.

Chapter 4. Vector-Valued Functions

a. Period0
b. Thing
c. Undefined
d. Undefined

59. The _____ is an imaginary line on the Earth's surface equidistant from the North Pole and South Pole.
   a. Thing
   b. Equator0
   c. Undefined
   d. Undefined

60. Isaac Newton's _____ states the following: Every single point mass attracts every other point mass by a force pointing along the line combining the two.
   a. Thing
   b. Law of gravitation0
   c. Undefined
   d. Undefined

61. The _____ is defined as the summation of all particles and energy that exist and the space-time which all events occur.
   a. Universe0
   b. Thing
   c. Undefined
   d. Undefined

62. A _____ signifies a point or points of probability on a subject e.g., the _____ of creativity, which allows for the formation of rule or norm or law by interpretation of the phenomena events that can be created.
   a. Principle0
   b. Thing
   c. Undefined
   d. Undefined

63. Leonhard _____ was a pioneering Swiss mathematician and physicist, who spent most of his life in Russia and Germany.
   a. Euler0
   b. Person
   c. Undefined
   d. Undefined

64. Sir _____ was an Irish mathematician, physicist, and astronomer who made important contributions to the development of optics, dynamics, and algebra. His discovery of quaternions is perhaps his best known investigation.
   a. Person
   b. William Rowan Hamilton0
   c. Undefined
   d. Undefined

65. _____, Greek for "knowledge of nature," is the branch of science concerned with the discovery and characterization of universal laws which govern matter, energy, space, and time.
   a. Thing
   b. Physics0
   c. Undefined
   d. Undefined

66. The _____ of an object is the extra energy which it possesses due to its motion.
   a. Thing
   b. Kinetic energy0
   c. Undefined
   d. Undefined

67. In physics, a _____ may refer to the scalar _____ or to the vector _____.
   a. Potential0
   b. Thing
   c. Undefined
   d. Undefined

Chapter 4. Vector-Valued Functions

68. The plus and _____ signs are mathematical symbols used to represent the notions of positive and negative as well as the operations of addition and subtraction.
   a. Thing
   b. Minus0
   c. Undefined
   d. Undefined

69. _____ is a set, with some particular properties and usually some additional structure, such as the operations of addition or multiplication, for instance.
   a. Space0
   b. Thing
   c. Undefined
   d. Undefined

70. _____ is the path a moving object follows through space.
   a. Thing
   b. Projectile motion0
   c. Undefined
   d. Undefined

71. A _____ is a unit of length in the metric system, equal to one thousand metres, the current SI base unit of length
   a. Thing
   b. Kilometer0
   c. Undefined
   d. Undefined

72. The _____ of measurement are a globally standardized and modernized form of the metric system.
   a. Units0
   b. Thing
   c. Undefined
   d. Undefined

73. The _____ or kilogramme is the SI base unit of mass. It is defined as being equal to the mass of the international prototype of the _____.
   a. Thing
   b. Kilogram0
   c. Undefined
   d. Undefined

74. The metre (or _____, see spelling differences) is a measure of length. It is the basic unit of length in the metric system and in the International System of Units (SI), used around the world for general and scientific purposes.
   a. Concept
   b. Meter0
   c. Undefined
   d. Undefined

75. In Euclidean geometry, an _____ is a closed segment of a differentiable curve in the two-dimensional plane; for example, a circular _____ is a segment of a circle.
   a. Arc0
   b. Concept
   c. Undefined
   d. Undefined

76. _____ is the transport of people on a trip/journey or the process or time involved in a person or object moving from one location to another.
   a. Thing
   b. Travel0
   c. Undefined
   d. Undefined

77. _____ also called rectification of a curve—was historically difficult.
   a. Arc length0
   b. Thing
   c. Undefined
   d. Undefined

78. In elementary algebra, an _____ is a set that contains every real number between two indicated numbers and may contain the two numbers themselves.
   a. Thing
   b. Interval0
   c. Undefined
   d. Undefined

79. A _____ is a function that assigns a number to subsets of a given set.
   a. Measure0
   b. Thing
   c. Undefined
   d. Undefined

80. The _____ is the distance around a closed curve. _____ is a kind of perimeter.
   a. Circumference0
   b. Thing
   c. Undefined
   d. Undefined

81. In mathematical analysis and related areas of mathematics, a set is called _____, if it is, in a certain sense, of finite size.
   a. Bounded0
   b. Thing
   c. Undefined
   d. Undefined

82. In mathematics, a set is called _____ if there is a bijection between the set and some set of the form {1, 2, ..., n} where n is a natural number.
   a. Thing
   b. Finite0
   c. Undefined
   d. Undefined

83. A _____ function is a function for which, intuitively, small changes in the input result in small changes in the output.
   a. Event
   b. Continuous0
   c. Undefined
   d. Undefined

84. A _____ defined function f(x) of a real variable x is a function whose definition is given differently on disjoint subsets of its domain.
   a. Piecewise0
   b. Thing
   c. Undefined
   d. Undefined

85. A _____ is a set of numbers that designate location in a given reference system, such as x,y in a planar _____ system or an x,y,z in a three-dimensional _____ system.
   a. Thing
   b. Coordinate0
   c. Undefined
   d. Undefined

86. An _____ is a straight line around which a geometric figure can be rotated.
   a. Axis0
   b. Thing
   c. Undefined
   d. Undefined

87. In mathematics, a _____ of a number x is a number r such that $r^2 = x$, or in words, a number r whose square (the result of multiplying the number by itself) is x.

a. Thing
c. Undefined
b. Square root0
d. Undefined

88. _____ is a function that extends the concept of an ordinary sum
a. Thing
c. Undefined
b. Integrand0
d. Undefined

89. In mathematics, a _____ of a complex-valued function f is a member x of the domain of f such that f(x) vanishes at x, that is, x : f (x) = 0.
a. Thing
c. Undefined
b. Root0
d. Undefined

90. In geometry, a line _____ is a part of a line that is bounded by two end points, and contains every point on the line between its end points.
a. Concept
c. Undefined
b. Segment0
d. Undefined

91. A _____ is a part of a line that is bounded by two end points, and contains every point on the line between its end points.
a. Thing
c. Undefined
b. Line segment0
d. Undefined

92. In mathematics, a _____ is an ordered list of objects. Like a set, it contains members, also called elements or terms, and the number of terms is called the length of the _____. Unlike a set, order matters, and the exact same elements can appear multiple times at different positions in the _____.
a. Sequence0
c. Undefined
b. Thing
d. Undefined

93. A _____ is a symbolic representation denoting a quantity or expression. It often represents an "unknown" quantity that has the potential to change.
a. Thing
c. Undefined
b. Variable0
d. Undefined

94. In mathematics, _____ refers to a number of loosely related concepts in different areas of geometry. Intuitively, _____ is the amount by which a geometric object deviates from being flat, but this is defined in different ways depending on the context
a. Thing
c. Undefined
b. Curvature0
d. Undefined

95. _____ in a normed vector space is a vector whose length, or magnitude is 1.
a. Unit vector0
c. Undefined
b. Thing
d. Undefined

96. In abstract algebra, the term _____ refers to a number of concepts related to elements of finite order in groups and to the failure of modules to be free.

Chapter 4. Vector-Valued Functions

a. Torsion0
b. Thing
c. Undefined
d. Undefined

97. A _____ of a number is the product of that number with any integer.
a. Multiple0
b. Thing
c. Undefined
d. Undefined

98. In mathematics, _____ is synonymous with perpendicular when used as a simple adjective that is not part of any longer phrase with a standard definition. It means at right angles. It comes from the Greek ά½€ϊ Ι̂,ϊŒϊ, orthos, meaning "straight", used by Euclid to mean right; and ί³ϊ‰ί½ί¯ί± gonia, meaning angle. Two streets that cross each other at a right angle are _____ to one another.
a. Thing
b. Orthogonal0
c. Undefined
d. Undefined

99. A _____ is the quantity that defines certain relatively constant characteristics of systems or functions..
a. Thing
b. Parameter0
c. Undefined
d. Undefined

100. A _____ fraction is a fraction in which the absolute value of the numerator is less than the denominator--hence, the absolute value of the fraction is less than 1.
a. Thing
b. Proper0
c. Undefined
d. Undefined

101. _____ is electromagnetic radiation with a wavelength that is visible to the eye (visible _____) or, in a technical or scientific context, electromagnetic radiation of any wavelength.
a. Thing
b. Light0
c. Undefined
d. Undefined

102. A _____ is one of the basic shapes of geometry: a polygon with three vertices and three sides which are straight line segments.
a. Triangle0
b. Thing
c. Undefined
d. Undefined

103. _____ is the theorem stating that for any triangle, the measure of a given side must be less than the sum of the other two sides but greater than the difference between the two sides.
a. Triangle inequality0
b. Thing
c. Undefined
d. Undefined

104. Mathematical _____ is used to represent ideas.
a. Thing
b. Notation0
c. Undefined
d. Undefined

105. In mathematics, an _____ is a statement about the relative size or order of two objects.
a. Thing
b. Inequality0
c. Undefined
d. Undefined

Chapter 4. Vector-Valued Functions

106. In mathematics, a _____ (also spelled reflexion) is a map that transforms an object into its mirror image.
 a. Concept
 b. Reflection0
 c. Undefined
 d. Undefined

107. _____, also known as _____ of Alexandria, was a Greek mathematician. His Elements is the most successful textbook in the history of mathematics. In it, the principles of geometry are deduced from a small set of axioms. His method of proving mathematical theorems by logical reasoning from accepted first principles remains the backbone of mathematics and is responsible for the field's characteristic rigor
 a. Euclid0
 b. Person
 c. Undefined
 d. Undefined

108. In geometry, the relations of _____ are those such as 'lies on' between points and lines (as in 'point P lies on line L'), and 'intersects' (as in 'line L_1 intersects line L_2', in three-dimensional space). That is, they are the binary relations describing how subsets meet.
 a. Thing
 b. Incidence0
 c. Undefined
 d. Undefined

109. In mathematics, a _____ is a demonstration that, assuming certain axioms, some statement is necessarily true.
 a. Proof0
 b. Thing
 c. Undefined
 d. Undefined

110. In mathematics and physics, a _____ associates a scalar value, which can be either mathematical in definition, or physical, to every point in space.
 a. Thing
 b. Scalar field0
 c. Undefined
 d. Undefined

111. The _____ of a mathematical object is its size: a property by which it can be larger or smaller than other objects of the same kind; in technical terms, an ordering of the class of objects to which it belongs.
 a. Thing
 b. Magnitude0
 c. Undefined
 d. Undefined

112. _____ is a physical property of a system that underlies the common notions of hot and cold; something that is hotter has the greater _____.
 a. Thing
 b. Temperature0
 c. Undefined
 d. Undefined

113. _____ is the weakest of the four fundamental forces of bature, as described by Issac Newton
 a. Thing
 b. Gravitational force0
 c. Undefined
 d. Undefined

114. In the field of electromagnetism, _____ is usually the integral of a vector quantity over a finite surface.
 a. Thing
 b. Flux0
 c. Undefined
 d. Undefined

Chapter 4. Vector-Valued Functions

115. In mathematics and its applications, a _____ is a system for assigning an n-tuple of numbers or scalars to each point in an n-dimensional space.
   a. Coordinate system0
   b. Concept
   c. Undefined
   d. Undefined

116. In mathematics, an inequality is a statement about the relative size or order of two objects. For example 14 > 10, or 14 is _____ 10.
   a. Greater than0
   b. Thing
   c. Undefined
   d. Undefined

117. In mathematics, a _____ of a k-place relation $L \subseteq X_1 \times ... \times X_k$ is one of the sets X_j, $1 \leq j \leq k$. In the special case where k = 2 and $L \subseteq X_1 \times X_2$ is a function $L : X_1 \rightarrow X_2$, it is conventional to refer to X_1 as the _____ of the function and to refer to X_2 as the codomain of the function.
   a. Thing
   b. Domain0
   c. Undefined
   d. Undefined

118. _____ of a function of several variables is its derivative with respect to one of those variables with the others held constant as opposed to the total derivative, in which all variables are allowed to vary.
   a. Thing
   b. Partial derivative0
   c. Undefined
   d. Undefined

119. For a given gravitational field and a given position, the _____ is the minimum speed an object without propulsion needs to have to move away indefinitely from the source of the field, as opposed to falling back or staying in an orbit within a bounded distance from the source.
   a. Thing
   b. Escape velocity0
   c. Undefined
   d. Undefined

120. A _____ is a vehicle, missile or aircraft which obtains thrust by the reaction to the ejection of fast moving fluid from within a _____ engine.
   a. Thing
   b. Rocket0
   c. Undefined
   d. Undefined

121. A _____ is a deliberate process for transforming one or more inputs into one or more results.
   a. Calculation0
   b. Thing
   c. Undefined
   d. Undefined

122. The _____, the average in everyday English, which is also called the arithmetic _____ (and is distinguished from the geometric _____ or harmonic _____). The average is also called the sample _____. The expected value of a random variable, which is also called the population _____.
   a. Mean0
   b. Thing
   c. Undefined
   d. Undefined

123. In fluid dynamics the flow velocity, or _____, of a fluid is a vector field which is used to mathematically describe the motion of the fluid.

Chapter 4. Vector-Valued Functions

    a. Thing
    b. Velocity field0
    c. Undefined
    d. Undefined

124. In mathematics, the _____(e) for L-functions are a class of summation formulae, expressing sums taken over the complex number zeroes of a given L-function, typically in terms of quantities studied by number theory by use of the theory of special functions.
    a. Thing
    b. Explicit formula0
    c. Undefined
    d. Undefined

125. In mathematics, a _____ is a countable collection of open covers of a topological space that satisfies certain separation axioms.
    a. Development0
    b. Thing
    c. Undefined
    d. Undefined

126. _____ is the fee paid on borrowed money.
    a. Thing
    b. Interest0
    c. Undefined
    d. Undefined

127. _____ is an adjective usually refering to being in the centre.
    a. Central0
    b. Thing
    c. Undefined
    d. Undefined

128. In mathematics, the word _____ is used informally to refer to certain distinct bodies of knowledge about mathematics.
    a. Thing
    b. Theoretical0
    c. Undefined
    d. Undefined

129. In vector calculus, _____ is a vector differential operator. It is a mathematical tool serving primarily as a convention for mathematical notation; it makes many equations easier to comprehend, write, and remember. Mathematically, the _____ can be viewed as the derivative in multi-dimensional space.
    a. Thing
    b. Del operator0
    c. Undefined
    d. Undefined

130. The _____ of a solid object is the three-dimensional concept of how much space it occupies, often quantified numerically.
    a. Volume0
    b. Thing
    c. Undefined
    d. Undefined

131. An _____ of a product of sums expresses it as a sum of products by using the fact that multiplication distributes over addition.
    a. Expansion0
    b. Thing
    c. Undefined
    d. Undefined

132. In mathematics, science including computer science, linguistics and engineering, an _____ is, generally speaking, an independent variable or input to a function.

Chapter 4. Vector-Valued Functions

a. Argument0
b. Thing
c. Undefined
d. Undefined

133. In mathematics, a _____ is a statement that can be proved on the basis of explicitly stated or previously agreed assumptions.
   a. Theorem0
   b. Thing
   c. Undefined
   d. Undefined

134. In mathematics and logic, a _____ proof is a way of showing the truth or falsehood of a given statement by a straightforward combination of established facts, usually existing lemmas and theorems, without making any further assumptions.
   a. Thing
   b. Direct0
   c. Undefined
   d. Undefined

135. In geometry, a _____ is defined as a quadrilateral where all four of its angles are right angles.
   a. Thing
   b. Rectangle0
   c. Undefined
   d. Undefined

136. A _____ is a movement of an object in a circular motion. A two-dimensional object rotates around a center (or point) of _____. A three-dimensional object rotates around a line called an axis. If the axis of _____ is within the body, the body is said to rotate upon itself, or spin—which implies relative speed and perhaps free-movement with angular momentum. A circular motion about an external point, e.g. the Earth about the Sun, is called an orbit or more properly an orbital revolution.
   a. Thing
   b. Rotation0
   c. Undefined
   d. Undefined

137. In physics, the _____ momentum of an object rotating about some reference point is the measure of the extent to which the object will continue to rotate about that point unless acted upon by an external torque.
   a. Angular0
   b. Thing
   c. Undefined
   d. Undefined

138. _____ is a scalar measure of rotation rate. It is the magnitude of the vector quantity angular velocity.
   a. Angular frequency0
   b. Thing
   c. Undefined
   d. Undefined

139. _____ is a scalar measure of rotation rate. It is the magnitude of the vector quantity angular velocity.
   a. Angular speed0
   b. Thing
   c. Undefined
   d. Undefined

140. In physics, the _____ is a vector quantity (more precisely, a pseudovector) which specifies the angular speed at which an object is rotating along with the direction in which it is rotating.
   a. Thing
   b. Angular velocity0
   c. Undefined
   d. Undefined

141. In mathematics, suppose C is a collection of mathematical objects . Then we say that C is _____ if every c ∊ C is uniquely determined by less information about c than one would expect.

Chapter 4. Vector-Valued Functions

a. Rigid0
b. Thing
c. Undefined
d. Undefined

142. In linear algebra and geometry, a rotation (_____) is a type of transformation from one system of coordinates to another system of coordinates such that distance between any two points remains invariant under the transformation.
a. Thing
b. Rotational0
c. Undefined
d. Undefined

143. _____ is a vector field whose curl is zero.
a. Conservative vector field0
b. Thing
c. Undefined
d. Undefined

144. Two mathematical objects are equal if and only if they are precisely the same in every way. This defines a binary relation, _____, denoted by the sign of _____ "=" in such a way that the statement "x = y" means that x and y are equal.
a. Equality0
b. Thing
c. Undefined
d. Undefined

145. In mathematics, a _____ is a constant multiplicative factor of a certain object. The object can be such things as a variable, a vector, a function, etc. For example, the _____ of $9x^2$ is 9.
a. Coefficient0
b. Thing
c. Undefined
d. Undefined

146. An _____ is an equality that remains true regardless of the values of any variables that appear within it, to distinguish it from an equality which is true under more particular conditions.
a. Thing
b. Identity0
c. Undefined
d. Undefined

147. An _____ is a combination of numbers, operators, grouping symbols and/or free variables and bound variables arranged in a meaningful way which can be evaluated..
a. Expression0
b. Thing
c. Undefined
d. Undefined

148. The deductive-nomological model is a formalized view of scientific _____ in natural language.
a. Explanation0
b. Thing
c. Undefined
d. Undefined

149. _____ denotes the approach toward a definite value, as time goes on; or to a definite point, a common view or opinion, or toward a fixed or equilibrium state.
a. Thing
b. Convergence0
c. Undefined
d. Undefined

150. A _____ is a three-dimensional solid object bounded by six square faces, facets, or sides, with three meeting at each vertex.

Chapter 4. Vector-Valued Functions

    a. Cube0
    b. Thing
    c. Undefined
    d. Undefined

151. _____ was a German mathematician and philosopher. He invented calculus independently of Newton, and his notation is the one in general use since.
    a. Leibniz0
    b. Person
    c. Undefined
    d. Undefined

152. _____ is a kind of property which exists as magnitude or multitude. It is among the basic classes of things along with quality, substance, change, and relation.
    a. Amount0
    b. Thing
    c. Undefined
    d. Undefined

153. In mathematics, the conjugate _____ or adjoint matrix of an m-by-n matrix A with complex entries is the n-by-m matrix A* obtained from A by taking the transpose and then taking the complex conjugate of each entry.
    a. Thing
    b. Pairs0
    c. Undefined
    d. Undefined

154. In topology and related areas of mathematics a _____ or Moore-Smith sequence is a generalization of a sequence, intended to unify the various notions of limit and generalize them to arbitrary topological spaces.
    a. Thing
    b. Net0
    c. Undefined
    d. Undefined

155. In botany, _____ are above-ground plant organs specialized for photosynthesis. Their characteristics are typically analyzed by using Fiobonacci's sequences.
    a. Leaves0
    b. Thing
    c. Undefined
    d. Undefined

156. In mathematics, a _____ is the end result of a division problem. It can also be expressed as the number of times the divisor divides into the dividend.
    a. Thing
    b. Quotient0
    c. Undefined
    d. Undefined

157. _____ is mass m per unit volume V.
    a. Density0
    b. Thing
    c. Undefined
    d. Undefined

158. A _____ consists either of a suggested explanation for a phenomenon or of a reasoned proposal suggesting a possible correlation between multiple phenomena.
    a. Thing
    b. Hypothesis0
    c. Undefined
    d. Undefined

159. A _____ is the curve defined by the path of a point on the edge of circular wheel as the wheel rolls along a straight line.

Chapter 4. Vector-Valued Functions

a. Thing
b. Cycloid0
c. Undefined
d. Undefined

160. In mathematics, a _____ is the set of all points in three-dimensional space (R^3) which are at distance r from a fixed point of that space, where r is a positive real number called the radius of the _____. The fixed point is called the center or centre, and is not part of the _____ itself.
   a. Sphere0
   b. Thing
   c. Undefined
   d. Undefined

161. In mathematics, in the field of differential equations, an initial value problem is a differential equation together with specified value, called the _____, of the unknown function at a given point in the domain of the solution.
   a. Thing
   b. Initial condition0
   c. Undefined
   d. Undefined

162. _____ statistics are statistics that estimate population parameters.
   a. Parametric0
   b. Thing
   c. Undefined
   d. Undefined

163. In mathematics, the _____ of two sets A and B is the set that contains all elements of A that also belong to B (or equivalently, all elements of B that also belong to A), but no other elements.
   a. Intersection0
   b. Thing
   c. Undefined
   d. Undefined

164. _____ is the interdisciplinary scientific study of the atmosphere that focuses on weather processes and forecasting.
   a. Meteorology0
   b. Thing
   c. Undefined
   d. Undefined

165. In mathematics, two quantities are called _____ if they vary in such a way that one of the quantities is a constant multiple of the other, or equivalently if they have a constant ratio.
   a. Proportional0
   b. Thing
   c. Undefined
   d. Undefined

166. In astronomy, geography, geometry and related sciences and contexts, a plane is said to be _____ at a given point if it is locally perpendicular to the gradient of the gravity field, i.e., with the direction of the gravitational force at that point.
   a. Thing
   b. Horizontal0
   c. Undefined
   d. Undefined

167. In mathematics, an _____ on a real vector space is a choice of which ordered bases are "positively" oriented, or right-handed, and which are "negatively" oriented, or left-handed.
   a. Thing
   b. Orientation0
   c. Undefined
   d. Undefined

168. A _____ is a negotiable instrument instructing a financial institution to pay a specific amount of a specific currency from a specific demand account held in the maker/depositor's name with that institution. Both the maker and payee may be natural persons or legal entities.

Chapter 4. Vector-Valued Functions

a. Check0
b. Thing
c. Undefined
d. Undefined

169. The _____ rule, also known as a slipstick, is a mechanical analog computer, consisting of at least two finely divided scales , most often a fixed outer pair and a movable inner one, with a sliding window called the cursor.
   a. Thing
   b. Slide0
   c. Undefined
   d. Undefined

170. In mathematics, a _____ is a quadric surface, with the following equation in Cartesian coordinates: $(x/_a)^2 + (y/_b)^2 = 1$.
   a. Cylinder0
   b. Thing
   c. Undefined
   d. Undefined

171. _____ is the force that opposes the relative motion or tendency toward such motion of two surfaces in contact.
   a. Thing
   b. Friction0
   c. Undefined
   d. Undefined

172. In mathematics, _____ are two-dimensional manifolds or surfaces that are perfectly flat.
   a. Thing
   b. Planes0
   c. Undefined
   d. Undefined

173. _____, usually denoted symbolically by the Greek letter phi, Î¦, gives the location of a place on Earth north or south of the equator. _____ is an angular measurement in degrees (marked with Â°) ranging from 0Â° at the Equator (low _____) to 90Â° at the poles (90Â° N for the North Pole or 90Â° S for the South Pole; high _____). The complementary angle of a _____ is called the colatitude.
   a. Latitude0
   b. Thing
   c. Undefined
   d. Undefined

Chapter 5. Double and Triple Integrals

1. _____ is a process of combining or accumulating. It may also refer to:
   - a. Integration0
   - b. Thing
   - c. Undefined
   - d. Undefined

2. A _____ is one of the basic shapes of geometry: a polygon with three vertices and three sides which are straight line segments.
   - a. Triangle0
   - b. Thing
   - c. Undefined
   - d. Undefined

3. In mathematics, a _____ is a demonstration that, assuming certain axioms, some statement is necessarily true.
   - a. Thing
   - b. Proof0
   - c. Undefined
   - d. Undefined

4. In geometry, a line _____ is a part of a line that is bounded by two end points, and contains every point on the line between its end points.
   - a. Concept
   - b. Segment0
   - c. Undefined
   - d. Undefined

5. In geometry, a _____ is a special kind of point, usually a corner of a polygon, polyhedron, or higher dimensional polytope. In the geometry of curves a _____ is a point of where the first derivative of curvature is zero. In graph theory, a _____ is the fundamental unit out of which graphs are formed
   - a. Vertex0
   - b. Thing
   - c. Undefined
   - d. Undefined

6. In geometry, a _____ planar shape or solid is one that encloses and "fits snugly" around another geometric shape or solid.
   - a. Thing
   - b. Circumscribed0
   - c. Undefined
   - d. Undefined

7. In mathematics, the _____ is a conic section generated by the intersection of a right circular conical surface and a plane parallel to a generating straight line of that surface. It can also be defined as locus of points in a plane which are equidistant from a given point.
   - a. Thing
   - b. Parabola0
   - c. Undefined
   - d. Undefined

8. A _____ is a four-sided plane figure that has two sets of opposite parallel sides.
   - a. Parallelogram0
   - b. Concept
   - c. Undefined
   - d. Undefined

9. The _____ of a solid object is the three-dimensional concept of how much space it occupies, often quantified numerically.
   - a. Thing
   - b. Volume0
   - c. Undefined
   - d. Undefined

10. A _____ is the result of the addition of a set of numbers. The numbers may be natural numbers, complex numbers, matrices, or still more complicated objects. An infinite _____ is a subtle procedure known as a series.

a. Thing
b. Sum0
c. Undefined
d. Undefined

11. The _____ of a function is an extension of the concept of a sum, and are identified or found through the use of integration.
a. Thing
b. Integral0
c. Undefined
d. Undefined

12. In mathematics, a _____ is an n-tuple with n being 3.
a. Triple0
b. Thing
c. Undefined
d. Undefined

13. In geometry, a _____ is defined as a quadrilateral where all four of its angles are right angles.
a. Thing
b. Rectangle0
c. Undefined
d. Undefined

14. _____ is a set, with some particular properties and usually some additional structure, such as the operations of addition or multiplication, for instance.
a. Thing
b. Space0
c. Undefined
d. Undefined

15. In mathematical analysis and related areas of mathematics, a set is called _____, if it is, in a certain sense, of finite size.
a. Bounded0
b. Thing
c. Undefined
d. Undefined

16. In mathematics, a _____ is a two-dimensional manifold or surface that is perfectly flat.
a. Thing
b. Plane0
c. Undefined
d. Undefined

17. In mathematics, _____ are two-dimensional manifolds or surfaces that are perfectly flat.
a. Thing
b. Planes0
c. Undefined
d. Undefined

18. _____ is a method for approximating the values of integrals.
a. Thing
b. Riemann sum0
c. Undefined
d. Undefined

19. The _____ integers are all the integers from zero on upwards.
a. Thing
b. Nonnegative0
c. Undefined
d. Undefined

20. The mathematical concept of a _____ expresses the intuitive idea of deterministic dependence between two quantities, one of which is viewed as primary and the other as secondary. A _____ then is a way to associate a unique output for each input of a specified type, for example, a real number or an element of a given set.

a. Thing
b. Function0
c. Undefined
d. Undefined

21. In mathematics and the mathematical sciences, a _____ is a fixed, but possibly unspecified, value. This is in contrast to a variable, which is not fixed.
    a. Constant0
    b. Thing
    c. Undefined
    d. Undefined

22. Generally, a _____ is a splitting of something into parts.
    a. Partition0
    b. Thing
    c. Undefined
    d. Undefined

23. _____ is a mathematical subject that includes the study of limits, derivatives, integrals, and power series and constitutes a major part of modern university curriculum.
    a. Calculus0
    b. Thing
    c. Undefined
    d. Undefined

24. A _____ function is a function for which, intuitively, small changes in the input result in small changes in the output.
    a. Event
    b. Continuous0
    c. Undefined
    d. Undefined

25. A _____ signifies a point or points of probability on a subject e.g., the _____ of creativity, which allows for the formation of rule or norm or law by interpretation of the phenomena events that can be created.
    a. Principle0
    b. Thing
    c. Undefined
    d. Undefined

26. In geometry, a _____ is the intersection of a body in 2-dimensional space with a line, or of a body in 3-dimensional space with a plane
    a. Thing
    b. Cross section0
    c. Undefined
    d. Undefined

27. A frame of _____ is a particular perspective from which the universe is observed.
    a. Thing
    b. Reference0
    c. Undefined
    d. Undefined

28. Bonaventura Francesco _____ was an Italian mathematician known for _____'s principle,
    a. Person
    b. Cavalieri0
    c. Undefined
    d. Undefined

29. In mathematics, _____ geometry was the traditional name for the geometry of three-dimensional Euclidean space — for practical purposes the kind of space we live in.
    a. Thing
    b. Solid0
    c. Undefined
    d. Undefined

Chapter 5. Double and Triple Integrals

30. _____ was an Italian physicist, mathematician, astronomer, and philosopher who is closely associated with the scientific revolution.
   a. Galileo Galilei0
   b. Person
   c. Undefined
   d. Undefined

31. Sir Isaac _____, was an English physicist, mathematician, astronomer, natural philosopher, and alchemist, regarded by many as the greatest figure in the history of science
   a. Person
   b. Newton0
   c. Undefined
   d. Undefined

32. _____ of Syracuse was an ancient Greek mathematician, physicist and engineer. In addition to making important discoveries in the field of mathematics and geometry, he is credited with producing machines that were well ahead of their time.
   a. Person
   b. Archimedes0
   c. Undefined
   d. Undefined

33. _____ was a German mathematician and philosopher. He invented calculus independently of Newton, and his notation is the one in general use since.
   a. Person
   b. Leibniz0
   c. Undefined
   d. Undefined

34. In mathematics, _____ refers to the rewriting of an expression into a simpler form.
   a. Thing
   b. Reduction0
   c. Undefined
   d. Undefined

35. An _____ is a straight line around which a geometric figure can be rotated.
   a. Thing
   b. Axis0
   c. Undefined
   d. Undefined

36. In geometry, two lines or planes if one falls on the other in such a way as to create congruent adjacent angles. The term may be used as a noun or adjective. Thus, referring to Figure 1, the line AB is the _____ to CD through the point B.
   a. Thing
   b. Perpendicular0
   c. Undefined
   d. Undefined

37. In plane geometry, a _____ is a polygon with four equal sides, four right angles, and parallel opposite sides. In algebra, the _____ of a number is that number multiplied by itself.
   a. Square0
   b. Thing
   c. Undefined
   d. Undefined

38. In statistics, a _____ measure is one which is measuring what is supposed to measure.
   a. Valid0
   b. Thing
   c. Undefined
   d. Undefined

39. In mathematics, a _____ is an ordered list of objects. Like a set, it contains members, also called elements or terms, and the number of terms is called the length of the _____. Unlike a set, order matters, and the exact same elements can appear multiple times at different positions in the _____.

a. Sequence0
b. Thing
c. Undefined
d. Undefined

40. In mathematics, a _____ is a statement that can be proved on the basis of explicitly stated or previously agreed assumptions.
   a. Thing
   b. Theorem0
   c. Undefined
   d. Undefined

41. In mathematics, a _____ of a k-place relation $L \subseteq X_1 \times ... \times X_k$ is one of the sets X_j, $1 \le j \le k$. In the special case where $k = 2$ and $L \subseteq X_1 \times X_2$ is a function $L : X_1 \to X_2$, it is conventional to refer to X_1 as the _____ of the function and to refer to X_2 as the codomain of the function.
   a. Thing
   b. Domain0
   c. Undefined
   d. Undefined

42. In geometry, an _____ is a point at which a line segment or ray terminates.
   a. Thing
   b. Endpoint0
   c. Undefined
   d. Undefined

43. In set theory and other branches of mathematics, the _____ of a collection of sets is the set that contains everything that belongs to any of the sets, but nothing else.
   a. Thing
   b. Union0
   c. Undefined
   d. Undefined

44. _____ are the basic objects of study in graph theory. Informally speaking, a graph is a set of objects called points, nodes, or vertices connected by links called lines or edges.
   a. Thing
   b. Graphs0
   c. Undefined
   d. Undefined

45. In mathematics, the concept of a _____ tries to capture the intuitive idea of a geometrical one-dimensional and continuous object. A simple example is the circle.
   a. Curve0
   b. Thing
   c. Undefined
   d. Undefined

46. In mathematics, _____ are the intuitive idea of a geometrical one-dimensional and continuous object.
   a. Curves0
   b. Thing
   c. Undefined
   d. Undefined

47. In mathematics, a set is called _____ if there is a bijection between the set and some set of the form {1, 2, ..., n} where n is a natural number.
   a. Thing
   b. Finite0
   c. Undefined
   d. Undefined

48. A _____ is a symbolic representation denoting a quantity or expression. It often represents an "unknown" quantity that has the potential to change.

Chapter 5. Double and Triple Integrals

a. Variable0
b. Thing
c. Undefined
d. Undefined

49. Equivalence is the condition of being _____ or essentially equal.
a. Thing
b. Equivalent0
c. Undefined
d. Undefined

50. In mathematics, an _____ is a statement about the relative size or order of two objects.
a. Inequality0
b. Thing
c. Undefined
d. Undefined

51. In mathematics, the _____ (or modulus) of a real number is its numerical value without regard to its sign.
a. Absolute value0
b. Thing
c. Undefined
d. Undefined

52. In number theory, the _____ of arithmetic (or unique factorization theorem) states that every natural number greater than 1 can be written as a unique product of prime numbers.
a. Concept
b. Fundamental theorem0
c. Undefined
d. Undefined

53. The _____, the average in everyday English, which is also called the arithmetic _____ (and is distinguished from the geometric _____ or harmonic _____). The average is also called the sample _____. The expected value of a random variable, which is also called the population _____.
a. Mean0
b. Thing
c. Undefined
d. Undefined

54. Mathematical _____ is used to represent ideas.
a. Notation0
b. Thing
c. Undefined
d. Undefined

55. In elementary algebra, an _____ is a set that contains every real number between two indicated numbers and may contain the two numbers themselves.
a. Interval0
b. Thing
c. Undefined
d. Undefined

56. In a mathematical proof or a syllogism, a _____ is a statement that is the logical consequence of preceding statements.
a. Conclusion0
b. Concept
c. Undefined
d. Undefined

57. _____ of calculus is the statement that the two central operations of calculus, differentiation and integration, are inverse operations: if a continuous function is first integrated and then differentiated, the original function is retrieved.
a. Fundamental Theorem of Calculus0
b. Thing
c. Undefined
d. Undefined

58. _____ is the state of being greater than any finite real or natural number, however large.

Chapter 5. Double and Triple Integrals

    a. Thing   b. Infinite0
    c. Undefined   d. Undefined

59. An _____ of a function f is a function F whose derivative is equal to f, i.e., F' = f.
    a. Antiderivative0   b. Thing
    c. Undefined   d. Undefined

60. In mathematics, a _____ is a countable collection of open covers of a topological space that satisfies certain separation axioms.
    a. Development0   b. Thing
    c. Undefined   d. Undefined

61. A _____ is traditionally an infinitesimally small change in a variable.
    a. Differential0   b. Thing
    c. Undefined   d. Undefined

62. A _____ is a mathematical equation for an unknown function of one or several variables which relates the values of the function itself and of its derivatives of various orders.
    a. Differential equation0   b. Thing
    c. Undefined   d. Undefined

63. Two mathematical objects are equal if and only if they are precisely the same in every way. This defines a binary relation, _____, denoted by the sign of _____ "=" in such a way that the statement "x = y" means that x and y are equal.
    a. Thing   b. Equality0
    c. Undefined   d. Undefined

64. _____ was an Italian mathematician, best known for Fubini's theorem.
    a. Guido Fubini0   b. Person
    c. Undefined   d. Undefined

65. One of the three formats applicable to a quadratic function is the _____ which is defined as $f = ax^2 + bx + c$.
    a. Thing   b. General form0
    c. Undefined   d. Undefined

66. In mathematics, a _____ number is a number which can be expressed as a ratio of two integers. Non-integer _____ numbers (commonly called fractions) are usually written as the vulgar fraction a / b, where b is not zero.
    a. Rational0   b. Thing
    c. Undefined   d. Undefined

67. In mathematics, an _____ number is any real number that is not a rational number- that is, it is a number which cannot be expressed as a fraction m/n, where m and n are integers.
    a. Thing   b. Irrational0
    c. Undefined   d. Undefined

68. In mathematics, _____ describes an entity with a limit.

Chapter 5. Double and Triple Integrals

a. Thing
b. Convergent0
c. Undefined
d. Undefined

69. A _____ is a set whose members are members of another set or a set contained within another set.
   a. Subset0
   b. Thing
   c. Undefined
   d. Undefined

70. _____ are groups whose members are members of another set or a set contained within another set.
   a. Subsets0
   b. Thing
   c. Undefined
   d. Undefined

71. Continuous functions are of utmost importance in mathematics and applications. However, not all functions are continuous. If a function is not continuous at a point in its domain, one says that it has a _____ there. The set of all points of _____ of a function may be a discrete set, a dense set, or even the entire domain of the function.
   a. Thing
   b. Discontinuity0
   c. Undefined
   d. Undefined

72. In Euclidean geometry, a _____ is the set of all points in a plane at a fixed distance, called the radius, from a given point, the center.
   a. Circle0
   b. Thing
   c. Undefined
   d. Undefined

73. In classical geometry, a _____ of a circle or sphere is any line segment from its center to its boundary. By extension, the _____ of a circle or sphere is the length of any such segment. The _____ is half the diameter. In science and engineering the term _____ of curvature is commonly used as a synonym for _____.
   a. Thing
   b. Radius0
   c. Undefined
   d. Undefined

74. In mathematics, an _____ .
   a. Ellipse0
   b. Thing
   c. Undefined
   d. Undefined

75. An _____ is when two lines intersect somewhere on a plane creating a right angle at intersection
   a. Axes0
   b. Thing
   c. Undefined
   d. Undefined

76. _____ is a trigonemtric function that is important when studying triangles and modeling periodic phenomena, among other applications.
   a. Thing
   b. Sine0
   c. Undefined
   d. Undefined

77. In business, particularly accounting, a _____ is the time intervals that the accounts, statement, payments, or other calculations cover.
   a. Period0
   b. Thing
   c. Undefined
   d. Undefined

Chapter 5. Double and Triple Integrals

78. A _____ is a three-dimensional geometric shape formed by straight lines through a fixed point (vertex) to the points of a fixed curve (directrix)
   a. Cone0
   b. Concept
   c. Undefined
   d. Undefined

79. A _____ consists of one quarter of the coordinate plane.
   a. Quadrant0
   b. Thing
   c. Undefined
   d. Undefined

80. An _____ is a combination of numbers, operators, grouping symbols and/or free variables and bound variables arranged in a meaningful way which can be evaluated..
   a. Thing
   b. Expression0
   c. Undefined
   d. Undefined

81. _____ is a function that extends the concept of an ordinary sum
   a. Thing
   b. Integrand0
   c. Undefined
   d. Undefined

82. An _____ is a type of quadric surface that is a higher dimensional analogue of an ellipse.
   a. Ellipsoid0
   b. Thing
   c. Undefined
   d. Undefined

83. _____ is a means of calculating the volume of a solid of revolution, when integrating along the axis of revolution. This method models the generated 3 dimensional shape as a "stack" of an infinite number of disks of infinitesimal thickness.
   a. Thing
   b. Disk method0
   c. Undefined
   d. Undefined

84. In geometry, a _____ is a three-dimensional figure formed by six parallelograms.
   a. Thing
   b. Parallelepiped0
   c. Undefined
   d. Undefined

85. In mathematics, science including computer science, linguistics and engineering, an _____ is, generally speaking, an independent variable or input to a function.
   a. Argument0
   b. Thing
   c. Undefined
   d. Undefined

86. _____ is a quadric
   a. Thing
   b. Paraboloid0
   c. Undefined
   d. Undefined

87. In mathematics, a _____ is a quadric surface, with the following equation in Cartesian coordinates: $(x/a)^2 + (y/b)^2 = 1$.
   a. Cylinder0
   b. Thing
   c. Undefined
   d. Undefined

Chapter 5. Double and Triple Integrals

88. An n-sided _____ is a polyhedron formed by connecting an n-sided polygonal base and a point, called the apex, by n triangular faces. In other words, it is a conic solid with polygonal base.
    a. Thing
    b. Pyramid0
    c. Undefined
    d. Undefined

89. In mathematics, a _____ is the set of all points in three-dimensional space (R^3) which are at distance r from a fixed point of that space, where r is a positive real number called the radius of the _____. The fixed point is called the center or centre, and is not part of the _____ itself.
    a. Thing
    b. Sphere0
    c. Undefined
    d. Undefined

90. In geometry, _____ lines are two lines that share one or more common points.
    a. Thing
    b. Intersecting0
    c. Undefined
    d. Undefined

91. In mathematics, the _____ of a coordinate system is the point where the axes of the system intersect.
    a. Thing
    b. Origin0
    c. Undefined
    d. Undefined

Chapter 6. The Change of Variables Formula and Applications of Integration

1. A _____ is a symbolic representation denoting a quantity or expression. It often represents an "unknown" quantity that has the potential to change.
   a. Thing
   b. Variable0
   c. Undefined
   d. Undefined

2. _____ is a process of combining or accumulating. It may also refer to:
   a. Thing
   b. Integration0
   c. Undefined
   d. Undefined

3. _____ is a mathematical subject that includes the study of limits, derivatives, integrals, and power series and constitutes a major part of modern university curriculum.
   a. Thing
   b. Calculus0
   c. Undefined
   d. Undefined

4. The _____ of a function is an extension of the concept of a sum, and are identified or found through the use of integration.
   a. Thing
   b. Integral0
   c. Undefined
   d. Undefined

5. In mathematics, a _____ is an n-tuple with n being 3.
   a. Triple0
   b. Thing
   c. Undefined
   d. Undefined

6. In geometry, a _____ is defined as a quadrilateral where all four of its angles are right angles.
   a. Rectangle0
   b. Thing
   c. Undefined
   d. Undefined

7. The mathematical concept of a _____ expresses the intuitive idea of deterministic dependence between two quantities, one of which is viewed as primary and the other as secondary. A _____ then is a way to associate a unique output for each input of a specified type, for example, a real number or an element of a given set.
   a. Function0
   b. Thing
   c. Undefined
   d. Undefined

8. A _____ is a set of numbers that designate location in a given reference system, such as x,y in a planar _____ system or an x,y,z in a three-dimensional _____ system.
   a. Thing
   b. Coordinate0
   c. Undefined
   d. Undefined

9. An _____ is an equality that remains true regardless of the values of any variables that appear within it, to distinguish it from an equality which is true under more particular conditions.
   a. Thing
   b. Identity0
   c. Undefined
   d. Undefined

10. In mathematics, _____ is a part of the set theoretic notion of function.
    a. Thing
    b. Image0
    c. Undefined
    d. Undefined

Chapter 6. The Change of Variables Formula and Applications of Integration

11. In functional analysis and related areas of mathematics the _____ set of a given subset of a vector space is a certain set in the dual space.
   - a. Thing
   - b. Polar0
   - c. Undefined
   - d. Undefined

12. In plane geometry, a _____ is a polygon with four equal sides, four right angles, and parallel opposite sides. In algebra, the _____ of a number is that number multiplied by itself.
   - a. Square0
   - b. Thing
   - c. Undefined
   - d. Undefined

13. In mathematics, the _____ of a coordinate system is the point where the axes of the system intersect.
   - a. Origin0
   - b. Thing
   - c. Undefined
   - d. Undefined

14. In mathematics, a _____ of a k-place relation $L \subseteq X_1 \times \ldots \times X_k$ is one of the sets X_j, $1 \leq j \leq k$. In the special case where k = 2 and $L \subseteq X_1 \times X_2$ is a function $L : X_1 \to X_2$, it is conventional to refer to X_1 as the _____ of the function and to refer to X_2 as the codomain of the function.
   - a. Thing
   - b. Domain0
   - c. Undefined
   - d. Undefined

15. In geometry, a _____ is a special kind of point, usually a corner of a polygon, polyhedron, or higher dimensional polytope. In the geometry of curves a _____ is a point of where the first derivative of curvature is zero. In graph theory, a _____ is the fundamental unit out of which graphs are formed
   - a. Vertex0
   - b. Thing
   - c. Undefined
   - d. Undefined

16. The word _____ comes from the Latin word linearis, which means created by lines.
   - a. Linear0
   - b. Thing
   - c. Undefined
   - d. Undefined

17. In mathematics, a _____ is a rectangular table of numbers or, more generally, a table consisting of abstract quantities that can be added and multiplied.
   - a. Thing
   - b. Matrix0
   - c. Undefined
   - d. Undefined

18. In mathematics, a _____ in elementary terms is any of a variety of different functions from geometry, such as rotations, reflections and translations.
   - a. Thing
   - b. Transformation0
   - c. Undefined
   - d. Undefined

19. In mathematics, a _____ is a two-dimensional manifold or surface that is perfectly flat.
   - a. Thing
   - b. Plane0
   - c. Undefined
   - d. Undefined

20. _____ of a function of several variables is its derivative with respect to one of those variables with the others held constant as opposed to the total derivative, in which all variables are allowed to vary.

Chapter 6. The Change of Variables Formula and Applications of Integration

a. Partial derivative0
b. Thing
c. Undefined
d. Undefined

21. The _____ is a measurement of how a function changes when the values of its inputs change.
    a. Derivative0
    b. Thing
    c. Undefined
    d. Undefined

22. In algebra, a _____ is a function depending on n that associates a scalar, det(A), to every $n \times n$ square matrix A.
    a. Thing
    b. Determinant0
    c. Undefined
    d. Undefined

23. In mathematics, _____ is an elementary arithmetic operation. When one of the numbers is a whole number, _____ is the repeated sum of the other number.
    a. Thing
    b. Multiplication0
    c. Undefined
    d. Undefined

24. In mathematics, a linear map also called a _____ or linear operator is a function between two vector spaces that preserves the operations of vector addition and scalar multiplication.
    a. Thing
    b. Linear transformation0
    c. Undefined
    d. Undefined

25. A _____, is a symbolized depiction of space which highlights relations between components of that space. Most usually a _____ is a two-dimensional, geometrically accurate representation of a three-dimensional space.
    a. Thing
    b. Map0
    c. Undefined
    d. Undefined

26. A _____ is a four-sided plane figure that has two sets of opposite parallel sides.
    a. Parallelogram0
    b. Concept
    c. Undefined
    d. Undefined

27. In mathematical analysis and related areas of mathematics, a set is called _____, if it is, in a certain sense, of finite size.
    a. Bounded0
    b. Thing
    c. Undefined
    d. Undefined

28. In statistics, a _____ measure is one which is measuring what is supposed to measure.
    a. Valid0
    b. Thing
    c. Undefined
    d. Undefined

29. _____ is a trigonemtric function that is important when studying triangles and modeling periodic phenomena, among other applications.
    a. Thing
    b. Sine0
    c. Undefined
    d. Undefined

30. _____ means of or relating to the French philosopher and mathematician René Descartes.

Chapter 6. The Change of Variables Formula and Applications of Integration

a. Thing
c. Undefined
b. Cartesian0
d. Undefined

31. In mathematics, the _____ (or modulus) of a real number is its numerical value without regard to its sign.
a. Thing
c. Undefined
b. Absolute value0
d. Undefined

32. A _____ fraction is a fraction in which the absolute value of the numerator is less than the denominator--hence, the absolute value of the fraction is less than 1.
a. Thing
c. Undefined
b. Proper0
d. Undefined

33. A _____ is the result of the addition of a set of numbers. The numbers may be natural numbers, complex numbers, matrices, or still more complicated objects. An infinite _____ is a subtle procedure known as a series.
a. Sum0
c. Undefined
b. Thing
d. Undefined

34. An _____ or member of a set is an object that when collected together make up the set.
a. Element0
c. Undefined
b. Thing
d. Undefined

35. In mathematics, a _____ is a demonstration that, assuming certain axioms, some statement is necessarily true.
a. Proof0
c. Undefined
b. Thing
d. Undefined

36. An _____ of a function f is a function F whose derivative is equal to f, i.e., F' = f.
a. Antiderivative0
c. Undefined
b. Thing
d. Undefined

37. In mathematics, a _____ is a statement that can be proved on the basis of explicitly stated or previously agreed assumptions.
a. Theorem0
c. Undefined
b. Thing
d. Undefined

38. In number theory, the _____ of arithmetic (or unique factorization theorem) states that every natural number greater than 1 can be written as a unique product of prime numbers.
a. Concept
c. Undefined
b. Fundamental theorem0
d. Undefined

39. _____ of calculus is the statement that the two central operations of calculus, differentiation and integration, are inverse operations: if a continuous function is first integrated and then differentiated, the original function is retrieved.
a. Thing
c. Undefined
b. Fundamental Theorem of Calculus0
d. Undefined

40. In calculus, the _____ is a formula for the derivative of the composite of two functions.

Chapter 6. The Change of Variables Formula and Applications of Integration

a. Chain rule0
b. Concept
c. Undefined
d. Undefined

41. In geometry, an _____ is a point at which a line segment or ray terminates.
   a. Endpoint0
   b. Thing
   c. Undefined
   d. Undefined

42. In common philosophical language, a proposition or _____, is the content of an assertion, that is, it is true-or-false and defined by the meaning of a particular piece of language.
   a. Statement0
   b. Concept
   c. Undefined
   d. Undefined

43. In elementary algebra, an _____ is a set that contains every real number between two indicated numbers and may contain the two numbers themselves.
   a. Interval0
   b. Thing
   c. Undefined
   d. Undefined

44. _____ is a function that extends the concept of an ordinary sum
   a. Thing
   b. Integrand0
   c. Undefined
   d. Undefined

45. In mathematics and logic, a _____ proof is a way of showing the truth or falsehood of a given statement by a straightforward combination of established facts, usually existing lemmas and theorems, without making any further assumptions.
   a. Thing
   b. Direct0
   c. Undefined
   d. Undefined

46. In mathematics, the concept of a _____ tries to capture the intuitive idea of a geometrical one-dimensional and continuous object. A simple example is the circle.
   a. Thing
   b. Curve0
   c. Undefined
   d. Undefined

47. In mathematics, a _____ number is a real or complex number which is not algebraic, that is, not a solution of a non-zero polynomial equation, with rational coefficients.
   a. Transcendental0
   b. Thing
   c. Undefined
   d. Undefined

48. In mathematics, _____ refers to the rewriting of an expression into a simpler form.
   a. Thing
   b. Reduction0
   c. Undefined
   d. Undefined

49. In mathematics, a _____ of a number x is a number r such that $r^2 = x$, or in words, a number r whose square (the result of multiplying the number by itself) is x.
   a. Square root0
   b. Thing
   c. Undefined
   d. Undefined

Chapter 6. The Change of Variables Formula and Applications of Integration

50. In mathematics, a _____ of a complex-valued function f is a member x of the domain of f such that f(x) vanishes at x, that is, x : f (x) = 0.
    a. Root0
    b. Thing
    c. Undefined
    d. Undefined

51. In physics and in _____ calculus, a spatial _____, or simply _____, is a concept characterized by a magnitude and a direction.
    a. Thing
    b. Vector0
    c. Undefined
    d. Undefined

52. The _____ of a solid object is the three-dimensional concept of how much space it occupies, often quantified numerically.
    a. Volume0
    b. Thing
    c. Undefined
    d. Undefined

53. In geometry, a _____ is a three-dimensional figure formed by six parallelograms.
    a. Thing
    b. Parallelepiped0
    c. Undefined
    d. Undefined

54. A _____ is a function that assigns a number to subsets of a given set.
    a. Thing
    b. Measure0
    c. Undefined
    d. Undefined

55. In set theory and other branches of mathematics, the _____ of a collection of sets is the set that contains everything that belongs to any of the sets, but nothing else.
    a. Thing
    b. Union0
    c. Undefined
    d. Undefined

56. A _____ function is a function for which, intuitively, small changes in the input result in small changes in the output.
    a. Continuous0
    b. Event
    c. Undefined
    d. Undefined

57. _____ are the basic objects of study in graph theory. Informally speaking, a graph is a set of objects called points, nodes, or vertices connected by links called lines or edges.
    a. Thing
    b. Graphs0
    c. Undefined
    d. Undefined

58. A _____ is a negotiable instrument instructing a financial institution to pay a specific amount of a specific currency from a specific demand account held in the maker/depositor's name with that institution. Both the maker and payee may be natural persons or legal entities.
    a. Thing
    b. Check0
    c. Undefined
    d. Undefined

59. An _____ is the limit of a definite integral, as an endpoint of the interval of integration approaches either a specified real number or ‡ or − ‡ or, in some cases, as both endpoints approach limits.

a. Improper integral0
b. Thing
c. Undefined
d. Undefined

60. A _____ is one of the basic shapes of geometry: a polygon with three vertices and three sides which are straight line segments.
   a. Triangle0
   b. Thing
   c. Undefined
   d. Undefined

61. In mathematics, a _____ is a quadric surface, with the following equation in Cartesian coordinates: $(x/_a)^2 + (y/_b)^2 = 1$.
   a. Thing
   b. Cylinder0
   c. Undefined
   d. Undefined

62. In mathematics, the _____ of Bernoulli is an eight-shaped algebraic curve described by a Cartesian equation
   a. Thing
   b. Lemniscate0
   c. Undefined
   d. Undefined

63. In mathematics, a _____ is the set of all points in three-dimensional space (R^3) which are at distance r from a fixed point of that space, where r is a positive real number called the radius of the _____. The fixed point is called the center or centre, and is not part of the _____ itself.
   a. Sphere0
   b. Thing
   c. Undefined
   d. Undefined

64. In mathematics, _____ geometry was the traditional name for the geometry of three-dimensional Euclidean space — for practical purposes the kind of space we live in.
   a. Thing
   b. Solid0
   c. Undefined
   d. Undefined

65. An _____ is a type of quadric surface that is a higher dimensional analogue of an ellipse.
   a. Ellipsoid0
   b. Thing
   c. Undefined
   d. Undefined

66. A _____ is a three-dimensional geometric shape formed by straight lines through a fixed point (vertex) to the points of a fixed curve (directrix)
   a. Concept
   b. Cone0
   c. Undefined
   d. Undefined

67. An _____ is one of eight divisions.
   a. Octant0
   b. Thing
   c. Undefined
   d. Undefined

68. An _____ is when two lines intersect somewhere on a plane creating a right angle at intersection
   a. Thing
   b. Axes0
   c. Undefined
   d. Undefined

Chapter 6. The Change of Variables Formula and Applications of Integration

69. In mathematics, an _____, mean, or central tendency of a data set refers to a measure of the "middle" or "expected" value of the data set.
    a. Average0
    b. Concept
    c. Undefined
    d. Undefined

70. In mathematics, two quantities are called _____ if they vary in such a way that one of the quantities is a constant multiple of the other, or equivalently if they have a constant ratio.
    a. Proportional0
    b. Thing
    c. Undefined
    d. Undefined

71. A _____ is a three-dimensional solid object bounded by six square faces, facets, or sides, with three meeting at each vertex.
    a. Thing
    b. Cube0
    c. Undefined
    d. Undefined

72. A _____ is a quantity that denotes the proportional amount or magnitude of one quantity relative to another.
    a. Thing
    b. Ratio0
    c. Undefined
    d. Undefined

73. _____ is a set, with some particular properties and usually some additional structure, such as the operations of addition or multiplication, for instance.
    a. Thing
    b. Space0
    c. Undefined
    d. Undefined

74. _____ is a physical property of a system that underlies the common notions of hot and cold; something that is hotter has the greater _____.
    a. Thing
    b. Temperature0
    c. Undefined
    d. Undefined

75. In mathematics and the mathematical sciences, a _____ is a fixed, but possibly unspecified, value. This is in contrast to a variable, which is not fixed.
    a. Thing
    b. Constant0
    c. Undefined
    d. Undefined

76. A _____ is the part of a fraction that tells how many equal parts make up a whole, and which is used in the name of the fraction: "halves", "thirds", "fourths" or "quarters", "fifths" and so on.
    a. Denominator0
    b. Concept
    c. Undefined
    d. Undefined

77. _____ is a special mathematical relationship between two quantities.Two quantities are called proportional if they vary in such a way that one of the quantities is a constant multiple of the other, or equivalently if they have a constant ratio.
    a. Proportionality0
    b. Thing
    c. Undefined
    d. Undefined

78. In geometry, the _____ of an object is a point in some sense in the middle of the object.

Chapter 6. The Change of Variables Formula and Applications of Integration

    a. Thing   b. Center0
    c. Undefined   d. Undefined

79. In physics, the _____ of a system of particles is a specific point at which, for many purposes, the system's mass behaves as if it were concentrated.
    a. Center of mass0   b. Thing
    c. Undefined   d. Undefined

80. _____ is the property of a physical object that quantifies the amount of matter and energy it is equivalent to.
    a. Thing   b. Mass0
    c. Undefined   d. Undefined

81. In banking and accountancy, the outstanding _____ is the amount of money owned, or due, that remains in a deposit account or a loan account at a given date, after all past remittances, payments and withdrawal have been accounted for.
    a. Thing   b. Balance0
    c. Undefined   d. Undefined

82. _____ is mass m per unit volume V.
    a. Density0   b. Thing
    c. Undefined   d. Undefined

83. A _____ is a numeral used to indicate a count. The most common use of the word today is to name the part of a fraction that tells the number or count of equal parts.
    a. Thing   b. Numerator0
    c. Undefined   d. Undefined

84. A _____ is a deliberate process for transforming one or more inputs into one or more results.
    a. Calculation0   b. Thing
    c. Undefined   d. Undefined

85. In mathematics, a _____ (also spelled reflexion) is a map that transforms an object into its mirror image.
    a. Reflection0   b. Concept
    c. Undefined   d. Undefined

86. _____ means "constancy", i.e. if something retains a certain feature even after we change a way of looking at it, then it is symmetric.
    a. Thing   b. Symmetry0
    c. Undefined   d. Undefined

87. An _____ is a straight line around which a geometric figure can be rotated.
    a. Thing   b. Axis0
    c. Undefined   d. Undefined

88. A _____ signifies a point or points of probability on a subject e.g., the _____ of creativity, which allows for the formation of rule or norm or law by interpretation of the phenomena events that can be created.

Chapter 6. The Change of Variables Formula and Applications of Integration

a. Principle0
b. Thing
c. Undefined
d. Undefined

89. _____ of Syracuse was an ancient Greek mathematician, physicist and engineer. In addition to making important discoveries in the field of mathematics and geometry, he is credited with producing machines that were well ahead of their time.
a. Person
b. Archimedes0
c. Undefined
d. Undefined

90. In economics, economic _____ is simply a state of the world where economic forces are balanced and in the absence of external influences the values of economic variables will not change.
a. Equilibrium0
b. Thing
c. Undefined
d. Undefined

91. _____, also known as _____ of Alexandria, was a Greek mathematician. His Elements is the most successful textbook in the history of mathematics. In it, the principles of geometry are deduced from a small set of axioms. His method of proving mathematical theorems by logical reasoning from accepted first principles remains the backbone of mathematics and is responsible for the field's characteristic rigor
a. Euclid0
b. Person
c. Undefined
d. Undefined

92. In mathematics, suppose C is a collection of mathematical objects . Then we say that C is _____ if every c ∈ C is uniquely determined by less information about c than one would expect.
a. Thing
b. Rigid0
c. Undefined
d. Undefined

93. In mathematics, a subset of Euclidean space R^n is called _____ if it is closed and bounded.
a. Thing
b. Compact0
c. Undefined
d. Undefined

94. A _____ is a movement of an object in a circular motion. A two-dimensional object rotates around a center (or point) of _____. A three-dimensional object rotates around a line called an axis. If the axis of _____ is within the body, the body is said to rotate upon itself, or spin—which implies relative speed and perhaps free-movement with angular momentum. A circular motion about an external point, e.g. the Earth about the Sun, is called an orbit or more properly an orbital revolution.
a. Thing
b. Rotation0
c. Undefined
d. Undefined

95. _____ is a quadric
a. Paraboloid0
b. Thing
c. Undefined
d. Undefined

96. In vector calculus, the _____ of a scalar field is a vector field which points in the direction of the greatest rate of increase of the scalar field, and whose magnitude is the greatest rate of change.

Chapter 6. The Change of Variables Formula and Applications of Integration

a. Thing
b. Gradient0
c. Undefined
d. Undefined

97. _____ is the weakest of the four fundamental forces of bature, as described by Issac Newton
a. Gravitational force0
b. Thing
c. Undefined
d. Undefined

98. In physics, a _____ may refer to the scalar _____ or to the vector _____.
a. Potential0
b. Thing
c. Undefined
d. Undefined

99. In physics, _____ is an influence that may cause an object to accelerate. It may be experienced as a lift, a push, or a pull. The actual acceleration of the body is determined by the vector sum of all forces acting on it, known as net _____ or resultant _____.
a. Force0
b. Thing
c. Undefined
d. Undefined

100. _____ algebra (sometimes called General algebra) is the field of mathematics that studies the ideas common to all algebraic structures.
a. Universal0
b. Thing
c. Undefined
d. Undefined

101. A _____ of a number is the product of that number with any integer.
a. Thing
b. Multiple0
c. Undefined
d. Undefined

102. Sir Isaac _____, was an English physicist, mathematician, astronomer, natural philosopher, and alchemist, regarded by many as the greatest figure in the history of science
a. Newton0
b. Person
c. Undefined
d. Undefined

103. _____ is a mathematical system attributed to the Greek mathematician Euclid of Alexandria.
a. Thing
b. Euclidean geometry0
c. Undefined
d. Undefined

104. A _____, as defined by the International Astronomical Union , is a celestial body orbiting a star or stellar remnant that is massive enough to be rounded by its own gravity, not massive enough to cause thermonuclear fusion in its core, and has cleared its neighboring region of planetesimals.
a. Planet0
b. Thing
c. Undefined
d. Undefined

105. In mathematics, an _____ is a statement about the relative size or order of two objects.
a. Thing
b. Inequality0
c. Undefined
d. Undefined

Chapter 6. The Change of Variables Formula and Applications of Integration 99

106. An _____ is a combination of numbers, operators, grouping symbols and/or free variables and bound variables arranged in a meaningful way which can be evaluated..
- a. Thing
- b. Expression0
- c. Undefined
- d. Undefined

107. In mathematics, _____ are two-dimensional manifolds or surfaces that are perfectly flat.
- a. Planes0
- b. Thing
- c. Undefined
- d. Undefined

108. In mathematics, the _____ of two sets A and B is the set that contains all elements of A that also belong to B (or equivalently, all elements of B that also belong to A), but no other elements.
- a. Intersection0
- b. Thing
- c. Undefined
- d. Undefined

109. _____ of an object is its speed in a particular direction.
- a. Velocity0
- b. Thing
- c. Undefined
- d. Undefined

110. In physics, the _____ momentum of an object rotating about some reference point is the measure of the extent to which the object will continue to rotate about that point unless acted upon by an external torque.
- a. Thing
- b. Angular0
- c. Undefined
- d. Undefined

111. In physics, the _____ is a vector quantity (more precisely, a pseudovector) which specifies the angular speed at which an object is rotating along with the direction in which it is rotating.
- a. Thing
- b. Angular velocity0
- c. Undefined
- d. Undefined

112. The _____ of an object is the extra energy which it possesses due to its motion.
- a. Thing
- b. Kinetic energy0
- c. Undefined
- d. Undefined

113. In logic, and especially in its applications to mathematics and philosophy, a _____ is an exception to a proposed general rule, i.e., a specific instance of the falsity of a universal quantification (a "for all" statement).
- a. Thing
- b. Counterexample0
- c. Undefined
- d. Undefined

114. In mathematics, defined and _____ are used to explain whether or not expressions have meaningful, sensible, and unambiguous values.
- a. Thing
- b. Undefined0
- c. Undefined
- d. Undefined

115. The _____ integers are all the integers from zero on upwards.
- a. Thing
- b. Nonnegative0
- c. Undefined
- d. Undefined

Chapter 6. The Change of Variables Formula and Applications of Integration

116. In classical geometry, a _____ of a circle or sphere is any line segment from its center to its boundary. By extension, the _____ of a circle or sphere is the length of any such segment. The _____ is half the diameter. In science and engineering the term _____ of curvature is commonly used as a synonym for _____.
a. Thing
b. Radius0
c. Undefined
d. Undefined

117. In mathematics, _____ describes an entity with a limit.
a. Thing
b. Convergent0
c. Undefined
d. Undefined

118. In geometry, a _____ (Greek words diairo = divide and metro = measure) of a circle is any straight line segment that passes through the centre and whose endpoints are on the circular boundary, or, in more modern usage, the length of such a line segment. When using the word in the more modern sense, one speaks of the _____ rather than a _____, because all diameters of a circle have the same length. This length is twice the radius. The _____ of a circle is also the longest chord that the circle has.
a. Diameter0
b. Thing
c. Undefined
d. Undefined

119. _____ is the state of being greater than any finite real or natural number, however large.
a. Infinite0
b. Thing
c. Undefined
d. Undefined

120. The metre (or _____, see spelling differences) is a measure of length. It is the basic unit of length in the metric system and in the International System of Units (SI), used around the world for general and scientific purposes.
a. Meter0
b. Concept
c. Undefined
d. Undefined

121. In mathematics, a _____ is the result of multiplying, or an expression that identifies factors to be multiplied.
a. Thing
b. Product0
c. Undefined
d. Undefined

122. In geometry, a _____ is the intersection of a body in 2-dimensional space with a line, or of a body in 3-dimensional space with a plane
a. Thing
b. Cross section0
c. Undefined
d. Undefined

123. In astronomy, geography, geometry and related sciences and contexts, a plane is said to be _____ at a given point if it is locally perpendicular to the gradient of the gravity field, i.e., with the direction of the gravitational force at that point.
a. Thing
b. Horizontal0
c. Undefined
d. Undefined

124. In mathematics, the _____ of continuity is a precise way to measure the smoothness of a function.
a. Thing
b. Modulus0
c. Undefined
d. Undefined

125. In Euclidean geometry, a _____ is the set of all points in a plane at a fixed distance, called the radius, from a given point, the center.
 a. Thing
 b. Circle0
 c. Undefined
 d. Undefined

126. In mathematics, a _____ of a number x is the exponent y of the power by such that $x = b^y$. The value used for the base b must be neither 0 nor 1, nor a root of 1 in the case of the extension to complex numbers, and is typically 10, e, or 2.
 a. Thing
 b. Logarithm0
 c. Undefined
 d. Undefined

127. _____, Greek for "knowledge of nature," is the branch of science concerned with the discovery and characterization of universal laws which govern matter, energy, space, and time.
 a. Physics0
 b. Thing
 c. Undefined
 d. Undefined

Chapter 7. Integrals Over Paths and Surfaces

1. _____ is a set, with some particular properties and usually some additional structure, such as the operations of addition or multiplication, for instance.
   a. Space0
   b. Thing
   c. Undefined
   d. Undefined

2. In mathematics, an _____, mean, or central tendency of a data set refers to a measure of the "middle" or "expected" value of the data set.
   a. Concept
   b. Average0
   c. Undefined
   d. Undefined

3. The _____ of a function is an extension of the concept of a sum, and are identified or found through the use of integration.
   a. Integral0
   b. Thing
   c. Undefined
   d. Undefined

4. In mathematics, the concept of a _____ tries to capture the intuitive idea of a geometrical one-dimensional and continuous object. A simple example is the circle.
   a. Curve0
   b. Thing
   c. Undefined
   d. Undefined

5. In mathematics, _____ refers to a number of loosely related concepts in different areas of geometry. Intuitively, _____ is the amount by which a geometric object deviates from being flat, but this is defined in different ways depending on the context
   a. Thing
   b. Curvature0
   c. Undefined
   d. Undefined

6. _____ is a physical property of a system that underlies the common notions of hot and cold; something that is hotter has the greater _____.
   a. Temperature0
   b. Thing
   c. Undefined
   d. Undefined

7. A _____ function is a function for which, intuitively, small changes in the input result in small changes in the output.
   a. Event
   b. Continuous0
   c. Undefined
   d. Undefined

8. A _____ number is a positive integer which has a positive divisor other than one or itself.
   a. Thing
   b. Composite0
   c. Undefined
   d. Undefined

9. A _____, formed by the composition of one function on another, represents the application of the former to the result of the application of the latter to the argument of the composite.
   a. Thing
   b. Composite function0
   c. Undefined
   d. Undefined

10. The mathematical concept of a _____ expresses the intuitive idea of deterministic dependence between two quantities, one of which is viewed as primary and the other as secondary. A _____ then is a way to associate a unique output for each input of a specified type, for example, a real number or an element of a given set.

Chapter 7. Integrals Over Paths and Surfaces

   a. Thing
   b. Function0
   c. Undefined
   d. Undefined

11. A _____ defined function $f(x)$ of a real variable x is a function whose definition is given differently on disjoint subsets of its domain.
   a. Thing
   b. Piecewise0
   c. Undefined
   d. Undefined

12. In Euclidean geometry, an _____ is a closed segment of a differentiable curve in the two-dimensional plane; for example, a circular _____ is a segment of a circle.
   a. Arc0
   b. Concept
   c. Undefined
   d. Undefined

13. _____ also called rectification of a curve—was historically difficult.
   a. Arc length0
   b. Thing
   c. Undefined
   d. Undefined

14. In mathematics and the mathematical sciences, a _____ is a fixed, but possibly unspecified, value. This is in contrast to a variable, which is not fixed.
   a. Thing
   b. Constant0
   c. Undefined
   d. Undefined

15. The _____, the average in everyday English, which is also called the arithmetic _____ (and is distinguished from the geometric _____ or harmonic _____). The average is also called the sample _____. The expected value of a random variable, which is also called the population _____.
   a. Thing
   b. Mean0
   c. Undefined
   d. Undefined

16. In mathematics, a _____ is a statement that can be proved on the basis of explicitly stated or previously agreed assumptions.
   a. Thing
   b. Theorem0
   c. Undefined
   d. Undefined

17. A _____ is the result of the addition of a set of numbers. The numbers may be natural numbers, complex numbers, matrices, or still more complicated objects. An infinite _____ is a subtle procedure known as a series.
   a. Sum0
   b. Thing
   c. Undefined
   d. Undefined

18. _____ is a method for approximating the values of integrals.
   a. Riemann sum0
   b. Thing
   c. Undefined
   d. Undefined

19. In mathematics, _____ are the intuitive idea of a geometrical one-dimensional and continuous object.
   a. Curves0
   b. Thing
   c. Undefined
   d. Undefined

Chapter 7. Integrals Over Paths and Surfaces

20. In mathematics, a _____ is a two-dimensional manifold or surface that is perfectly flat.
    a. Plane0
    b. Thing
    c. Undefined
    d. Undefined

21. In mathematics, a _____ is a curve in a Euclidian plane. The most frequently studied types are the smooth _____, and the algebraic _____.
    a. Plane curve0
    b. Thing
    c. Undefined
    d. Undefined

22. In mathematics, science including computer science, linguistics and engineering, an _____ is, generally speaking, an independent variable or input to a function.
    a. Thing
    b. Argument0
    c. Undefined
    d. Undefined

23. A _____ consists of one quarter of the coordinate plane.
    a. Thing
    b. Quadrant0
    c. Undefined
    d. Undefined

24. _____ is a trigonemtric function that is important when studying triangles and modeling periodic phenomena, among other applications.
    a. Sine0
    b. Thing
    c. Undefined
    d. Undefined

25. _____ is a process of combining or accumulating. It may also refer to:
    a. Thing
    b. Integration0
    c. Undefined
    d. Undefined

26. In linear algebra, real numbers are called scalars and relate to vectors in a vector space through the operation of _____ multiplication, in which a vector can be multiplied by a number to produce another vector.
    a. Scalar0
    b. Thing
    c. Undefined
    d. Undefined

27. In abstract algebra, the term _____ refers to a number of concepts related to elements of finite order in groups and to the failure of modules to be free.
    a. Thing
    b. Torsion0
    c. Undefined
    d. Undefined

28. In Euclidean geometry, a _____ is moving every point a constant distance in a specified direction.
    a. Concept
    b. Translation0
    c. Undefined
    d. Undefined

29. In mathematics, a _____ (also spelled reflexion) is a map that transforms an object into its mirror image.
    a. Concept
    b. Reflection0
    c. Undefined
    d. Undefined

Chapter 7. Integrals Over Paths and Surfaces

30. In mathematics, suppose C is a collection of mathematical objects . Then we say that C is _____ if every c ˛ C is uniquely determined by less information about c than one would expect.
    a. Thing
    b. Rigid0
    c. Undefined
    d. Undefined

31. A _____ is a movement of an object in a circular motion. A two-dimensional object rotates around a center (or point) of _____. A three-dimensional object rotates around a line called an axis. If the axis of _____ is within the body, the body is said to rotate upon itself, or spin—which implies relative speed and perhaps free-movement with angular momentum. A circular motion about an external point, e.g. the Earth about the Sun, is called an orbit or more properly an orbital revolution.
    a. Thing
    b. Rotation0
    c. Undefined
    d. Undefined

32. A _____ is traditionally an infinitesimally small change in a variable.
    a. Thing
    b. Differential0
    c. Undefined
    d. Undefined

33. _____ is the field dealing with differentiable functions on differentiable manifolds.
    a. Thing
    b. Differential geometry0
    c. Undefined
    d. Undefined

34. In Euclidean geometry, a _____ is the set of all points in a plane at a fixed distance, called the radius, from a given point, the center.
    a. Thing
    b. Circle0
    c. Undefined
    d. Undefined

35. In geometry, _____ lines are two lines that share one or more common points.
    a. Thing
    b. Intersecting0
    c. Undefined
    d. Undefined

36. In common philosophical language, a proposition or _____, is the content of an assertion, that is, it is true-or-false and defined by the meaning of a particular piece of language.
    a. Concept
    b. Statement0
    c. Undefined
    d. Undefined

37. A _____ is a method for fastening or securing linear material such as rope by tying or interweaving. It may consist of a length of one or more segments of rope, string, webbing, twine, strap or even chain interwoven so as to create in the line the ability to bind to itself or to some other object - the "load". Knots have been the subject of interest both for their ancient origins, common use, and the mathematical implications of _____ theory.
    a. Knot0
    b. Thing
    c. Undefined
    d. Undefined

38. In mathematics, _____ is the branch of topology that studies mathematical knots, which are defined as embeddings of a circle in 3-dimensional Euclidean space, R3.

Chapter 7. Integrals Over Paths and Surfaces

    a. Thing
    c. Undefined
    b. Knot theory0
    d. Undefined

39. A _____ is a set of numbers that designate location in a given reference system, such as x,y in a planar _____ system or an x,y,z in a three-dimensional _____ system.
    a. Thing
    c. Undefined
    b. Coordinate0
    d. Undefined

40. In functional analysis and related areas of mathematics the _____ set of a given subset of a vector space is a certain set in the dual space.
    a. Polar0
    c. Undefined
    b. Thing
    d. Undefined

41. The _____ is a measurement of how a function changes when the values of its inputs change.
    a. Thing
    c. Undefined
    b. Derivative0
    d. Undefined

42. In mathematics, a _____ is the set of all points in three-dimensional space (R^3) which are at distance r from a fixed point of that space, where r is a positive real number called the radius of the _____. The fixed point is called the center or centre, and is not part of the _____ itself.
    a. Thing
    c. Undefined
    b. Sphere0
    d. Undefined

43. _____ is the property of a physical object that quantifies the amount of matter and energy it is equivalent to.
    a. Thing
    c. Undefined
    b. Mass0
    d. Undefined

44. _____ is mass m per unit volume V.
    a. Thing
    c. Undefined
    b. Density0
    d. Undefined

45. In mathematics, the _____ of two sets A and B is the set that contains all elements of A that also belong to B (or equivalently, all elements of B that also belong to A), but no other elements.
    a. Thing
    c. Undefined
    b. Intersection0
    d. Undefined

46. _____ (Basel, July 27, 1667 - January 1, 1748) was a Swiss mathematician.
    a. Johann Bernoulli0
    c. Undefined
    b. Person
    d. Undefined

47. Sir Isaac _____, was an English physicist, mathematician, astronomer, natural philosopher, and alchemist, regarded by many as the greatest figure in the history of science
    a. Newton0
    c. Undefined
    b. Person
    d. Undefined

Chapter 7. Integrals Over Paths and Surfaces

48. A _____ is the curve defined by the path of a point on the edge of circular wheel as the wheel rolls along a straight line.
   a. Thing
   b. Cycloid0
   c. Undefined
   d. Undefined

49. _____ was an Italian physicist, mathematician, astronomer, and philosopher who is closely associated with the scientific revolution.
   a. Galileo Galilei0
   b. Person
   c. Undefined
   d. Undefined

50. Acid _____ ratio measures the ability of a company to use its near cash or quick assets to immediately extinguish its current liabilities.
   a. Thing
   b. Test0
   c. Undefined
   d. Undefined

51. In physics, _____ is an influence that may cause an object to accelerate. It may be experienced as a lift, a push, or a pull. The actual acceleration of the body is determined by the vector sum of all forces acting on it, known as net _____ or resultant _____.
   a. Force0
   b. Thing
   c. Undefined
   d. Undefined

52. In mathematics, a _____ is the result of multiplying, or an expression that identifies factors to be multiplied.
   a. Thing
   b. Product0
   c. Undefined
   d. Undefined

53. In physics and in _____ calculus, a spatial _____, or simply _____, is a concept characterized by a magnitude and a direction.
   a. Thing
   b. Vector0
   c. Undefined
   d. Undefined

54. The _____ of a mathematical object is its size: a property by which it can be larger or smaller than other objects of the same kind; in technical terms, an ordering of the class of objects to which it belongs.
   a. Thing
   b. Magnitude0
   c. Undefined
   d. Undefined

55. In mathematics, a set is called _____ if there is a bijection between the set and some set of the form {1, 2, ..., n} where n is a natural number.
   a. Thing
   b. Finite0
   c. Undefined
   d. Undefined

56. In mathematics, the _____, also known as the scalar product, is a binary operation which takes two vectors over the real numbers R and returns a real-valued scalar quantity. It is the standard inner product of the Euclidean space.
   a. Dot product0
   b. Thing
   c. Undefined
   d. Undefined

Chapter 7. Integrals Over Paths and Surfaces

57. In mathematics, the _____ of a function is the set of all "output" values produced by that function. Given a function $f : A \to B$, the _____ of f, is defined to be the set $\{x \in B : x = f(a) \text{ for some } a \in A\}$.
    a. Range0
    b. Thing
    c. Undefined
    d. Undefined

58. In elementary algebra, an _____ is a set that contains every real number between two indicated numbers and may contain the two numbers themselves.
    a. Interval0
    b. Thing
    c. Undefined
    d. Undefined

59. _____ is a construction in vector calculus which associates a vector to every point in a locally Euclidean space.
    a. Vector field0
    b. Thing
    c. Undefined
    d. Undefined

60. In mathematics, a _____ sometimes called a path integral is an integral where the function to be integrated is evaluated along a curve
    a. Thing
    b. Line integral0
    c. Undefined
    d. Undefined

61. In mathematics and applications, given a vector to a surface at a point, that vector can be decomposed uniquely as a sum of two vectors, one tangent to the surface, called the _____ of the vector.
    a. Thing
    b. Tangential component0
    c. Undefined
    d. Undefined

62. In mathematics, in the field of group theory, a _____ of a group is a quasisimple subnormal subgroup.
    a. Component0
    b. Concept
    c. Undefined
    d. Undefined

63. In mathematics, _____ is a part of the set theoretic notion of function.
    a. Image0
    b. Thing
    c. Undefined
    d. Undefined

64. In classical geometry, a _____ of a circle or sphere is any line segment from its center to its boundary. By extension, the _____ of a circle or sphere is the length of any such segment. The _____ is half the diameter. In science and engineering the term _____ of curvature is commonly used as a synonym for _____.
    a. Radius0
    b. Thing
    c. Undefined
    d. Undefined

65. In mathematics, an _____ on a real vector space is a choice of which ordered bases are "positively" oriented, or right-handed, and which are "negatively" oriented, or left-handed.
    a. Thing
    b. Orientation0
    c. Undefined
    d. Undefined

66. In calculus, the _____ is a formula for the derivative of the composite of two functions.

Chapter 7. Integrals Over Paths and Surfaces

   a. Chain rule0
   c. Undefined
   b. Concept
   d. Undefined

67. A _____ is a symbolic representation denoting a quantity or expression. It often represents an "unknown" quantity that has the potential to change.
   a. Variable0
   c. Undefined
   b. Thing
   d. Undefined

68. In geometry, a line _____ is a part of a line that is bounded by two end points, and contains every point on the line between its end points.
   a. Segment0
   c. Undefined
   b. Concept
   d. Undefined

69. In linear algebra, the _____ of an n-by-n square matrix A is defined to be the sum of the elements on the main diagonal of A,
   a. Thing
   c. Undefined
   b. Trace0
   d. Undefined

70. In vector calculus, the _____ of a scalar field is a vector field which points in the direction of the greatest rate of increase of the scalar field, and whose magnitude is the greatest rate of change.
   a. Gradient0
   c. Undefined
   b. Thing
   d. Undefined

71. A _____ signifies a point or points of probability on a subject e.g., the _____ of creativity, which allows for the formation of rule or norm or law by interpretation of the phenomena events that can be created.
   a. Principle0
   c. Undefined
   b. Thing
   d. Undefined

72. An _____ of a function f is a function F whose derivative is equal to f, i.e., F' = f.
   a. Thing
   c. Undefined
   b. Antiderivative0
   d. Undefined

73. _____ is a mathematical subject that includes the study of limits, derivatives, integrals, and power series and constitutes a major part of modern university curriculum.
   a. Thing
   c. Undefined
   b. Calculus0
   d. Undefined

74. In mathematics, a _____ is a connected curve that does not intersect itself and ends at the same point in which it starts.
   a. Closed curve0
   c. Undefined
   b. Thing
   d. Undefined

75. An _____ is a straight line around which a geometric figure can be rotated.
   a. Axis0
   c. Undefined
   b. Thing
   d. Undefined

76. _____ is a circle with a unit radius, i.e., a circle whose radius is 1.
   a. Unit circle0　　　　　　　　　　　　　　b. Thing
   c. Undefined　　　　　　　　　　　　　　　d. Undefined

77. Mathematical _____ is used to represent ideas.
   a. Notation0　　　　　　　　　　　　　　　b. Thing
   c. Undefined　　　　　　　　　　　　　　　d. Undefined

78. In plane geometry, a _____ is a polygon with four equal sides, four right angles, and parallel opposite sides. In algebra, the _____ of a number is that number multiplied by itself.
   a. Thing　　　　　　　　　　　　　　　　　b. Square0
   c. Undefined　　　　　　　　　　　　　　　d. Undefined

79. _____ is the distance around a given two-dimensional object. As a general rule, the _____ of a polygon can always be calculated by adding all the length of the sides together. So, the formula for triangles is P = a + b + c, where a, b and c stand for each side of it. For quadrilaterals the equation is P = a + b + c + d. For equilateral polygons, P = na, where n is the number of sides and a is the side length.
   a. Perimeter0　　　　　　　　　　　　　　 b. Thing
   c. Undefined　　　　　　　　　　　　　　　d. Undefined

80. In geometry, the _____ of an object is a point in some sense in the middle of the object.
   a. Thing　　　　　　　　　　　　　　　　　b. Center0
   c. Undefined　　　　　　　　　　　　　　　d. Undefined

81. In trigonometry, the _____ is a function defined as $\tan x = \sin x / \cos x$. The function is so-named because it can be defined as the length of a certain segment of a _____ (in the geometric sense) to the unit circle. In plane geometry, a line is _____ to a curve, at some point, if both line and curve pass through the point with the same direction.
   a. Tangent0　　　　　　　　　　　　　　　 b. Thing
   c. Undefined　　　　　　　　　　　　　　　d. Undefined

82. In the scientific method, an _____ (Latin: ex-+-periri, "of (or from) trying"), is a set of actions and observations, performed in the context of solving a particular problem or question, in order to support or falsify a hypothesis or research concerning phenomena.
   a. Experiment0　　　　　　　　　　　　　　b. Thing
   c. Undefined　　　　　　　　　　　　　　　d. Undefined

83. Equivalence is the condition of being _____ or essentially equal.
   a. Thing　　　　　　　　　　　　　　　　　b. Equivalent0
   c. Undefined　　　　　　　　　　　　　　　d. Undefined

84. In mathematics, the additive inverse, or _____ of a number n is the number that, when added to n, yields zero. The additive inverse of n is denoted −n. For example, 7 is −7, because 7 + (−7) = 0, and the additive inverse of −0.3 is 0.3, because −0.3 + 0.3 = 0.
   a. Thing　　　　　　　　　　　　　　　　　b. Opposite0
   c. Undefined　　　　　　　　　　　　　　　d. Undefined

Chapter 7. Integrals Over Paths and Surfaces

85. In mathematics, the _____ of a number n is the number that, when added to n, yields zero. The _____ of n is denoted −n. For example, 7 is −7, because 7 + (−7) = 0, and the _____ of −0.3 is 0.3, because −0.3 + 0.3 = 0.
   a. Thing
   b. Additive inverse0
   c. Undefined
   d. Undefined

86. In geometry, a _____ is a special kind of point, usually a corner of a polygon, polyhedron, or higher dimensional polytope. In the geometry of curves a _____ is a point of where the first derivative of curvature is zero. In graph theory, a _____ is the fundamental unit out of which graphs are formed
   a. Thing
   b. Vertex0
   c. Undefined
   d. Undefined

87. The _____ is the distance around a closed curve. _____ is a kind of perimeter.
   a. Circumference0
   b. Thing
   c. Undefined
   d. Undefined

88. A _____ is a landform that extends above the surrounding terrain in a limited area. A _____ is generally steeper than a hill, but there is no universally accepted standard definition for the height of a _____ or a hill although a _____ usually has an identifiable summit.
   a. Thing
   b. Mountain0
   c. Undefined
   d. Undefined

89. A _____ is a special kind of ratio, indicating a relationship between two measurements with different units, such as miles to gallons or cents to pounds.
   a. Rate0
   b. Thing
   c. Undefined
   d. Undefined

90. In mathematics, a _____ function in the sense of algebraic geometry is an everywhere-defined, polynomial function on an algebraic variety V with values in the field K over which V is defined.
   a. Thing
   b. Regular0
   c. Undefined
   d. Undefined

91. _____ element of an element x with respect to a binary operation * with identity element e is an element y such that x * y = y * x = e. In particular,
   a. Thing
   b. Inverse0
   c. Undefined
   d. Undefined

92. An _____ is a function which does the reverse of a given function.
   a. Inverse function0
   b. Thing
   c. Undefined
   d. Undefined

93. The _____ of a solid object is the three-dimensional concept of how much space it occupies, often quantified numerically.
   a. Volume0
   b. Thing
   c. Undefined
   d. Undefined

Chapter 7. Integrals Over Paths and Surfaces

94. _____, in economics and political economy, are the distributions or payments awarded to the various suppliers of the factors of production.
   a. Thing
   b. Returns0
   c. Undefined
   d. Undefined

95. A _____ is 360° or 2∂ radians.
   a. Turn0
   b. Thing
   c. Undefined
   d. Undefined

96. In mathematics, the _____ f is the collection of all ordered pairs . In particular, graph means the graphical representation of this collection, in the form of a curve or surface, together with axes, etc. Graphing on a Cartesian plane is sometimes referred to as curve sketching.
   a. Graph of a function0
   b. Thing
   c. Undefined
   d. Undefined

97. _____ are the basic objects of study in graph theory. Informally speaking, a graph is a set of objects called points, nodes, or vertices connected by links called lines or edges.
   a. Thing
   b. Graphs0
   c. Undefined
   d. Undefined

98. In mathematics, _____ are two-dimensional manifolds or surfaces that are perfectly flat.
   a. Planes0
   b. Thing
   c. Undefined
   d. Undefined

99. In geometry, a _____ is a surface of revolution generated by revolving a circle in three dimensional space about an axis coplanar with the circle, which does not touch the circle. Examples of tori include the surfaces of doughnuts and inner tubes. A circle rotated about a chord of the circle is called a _____ in some contexts, but this is not a common usage in mathematics. The shape produced when a circle is rotated about a chord resembles a round cushion. _____ was the Latin word for a cushion of this shape.
   a. Torus0
   b. Thing
   c. Undefined
   d. Undefined

100. Deductive _____ is the kind of _____ in which the conclusion is necessitated by, or reached from, previously known facts (the premises).
   a. Thing
   b. Reasoning0
   c. Undefined
   d. Undefined

101. In mathematics, a _____ is a quadric surface, with the following equation in Cartesian coordinates: $(x/_a)^2 + (y/_b)^2 = 1$.
   a. Cylinder0
   b. Thing
   c. Undefined
   d. Undefined

102. _____, a field in mathematics, is the study of how functions change when their inputs change. The primary object of study in _____ is the derivative.

Chapter 7. Integrals Over Paths and Surfaces

a. Thing
b. Differential calculus0
c. Undefined
d. Undefined

103. In mathematics, a _____ of a k-place relation $L \subseteq X_1 \times ... \times X_k$ is one of the sets X_j, $1 \leq j \leq k$. In the special case where k = 2 and $L \subseteq X_1 \times X_2$ is a function $L : X_1 \rightarrow X_2$, it is conventional to refer to X_1 as the _____ of the function and to refer to X_2 as the codomain of the function.

a. Thing
b. Domain0
c. Undefined
d. Undefined

104. A _____ is a negotiable instrument instructing a financial institution to pay a specific amount of a specific currency from a specific demand account held in the maker/depositor's name with that institution. Both the maker and payee may be natural persons or legal entities.

a. Check0
b. Thing
c. Undefined
d. Undefined

105. _____ is the study of terms and their use — of words and compound words that are used in specific contexts.

a. Terminology0
b. Thing
c. Undefined
d. Undefined

106. A _____ is a three-dimensional geometric shape formed by straight lines through a fixed point (vertex) to the points of a fixed curve (directrix)

a. Cone0
b. Concept
c. Undefined
d. Undefined

107. _____ in a normed vector space is a vector whose length, or magnitude is 1.

a. Unit vector0
b. Thing
c. Undefined
d. Undefined

108. An _____ is a combination of numbers, operators, grouping symbols and/or free variables and bound variables arranged in a meaningful way which can be evaluated..

a. Thing
b. Expression0
c. Undefined
d. Undefined

109. In mathematics, the _____ of a coordinate system is the point where the axes of the system intersect.

a. Thing
b. Origin0
c. Undefined
d. Undefined

110. In astronomy, geography, geometry and related sciences and contexts, a plane is said to be _____ at a given point if it is locally perpendicular to the gradient of the gravity field, i.e., with the direction of the gravitational force at that point.

a. Thing
b. Horizontal0
c. Undefined
d. Undefined

111. In mathamatics, a _____ is a quadric, a type of surface in three dimensions, described by the equation

a. Thing
b. Hyperboloid0
c. Undefined
d. Undefined

Chapter 7. Integrals Over Paths and Surfaces

112. A _____ is a part of a line that is bounded by two end points, and contains every point on the line between its end points.
    a. Line segment0
    b. Thing
    c. Undefined
    d. Undefined

113. The word _____ comes from the Latin word linearis, which means created by lines.
    a. Thing
    b. Linear0
    c. Undefined
    d. Undefined

114. _____ is an approximation of a general function using a linear function more precisely, an affine function.
    a. Thing
    b. Linear approximation0
    c. Undefined
    d. Undefined

115. In mathematics, an _____ is a generalization for the concept of a function in which the dependent variable may not be given explicitly in terms of the independent variable.
    a. Thing
    b. Implicit function0
    c. Undefined
    d. Undefined

116. In set theory and other branches of mathematics, the _____ of a collection of sets is the set that contains everything that belongs to any of the sets, but nothing else.
    a. Union0
    b. Thing
    c. Undefined
    d. Undefined

117. _____ is a function that extends the concept of an ordinary sum
    a. Integrand0
    b. Thing
    c. Undefined
    d. Undefined

118. _____ after the plane and the catenoid, is the third minimal surface to be known.
    a. Helicoid0
    b. Thing
    c. Undefined
    d. Undefined

119. In geometry, a _____ is the intersection of a body in 2-dimensional space with a line, or of a body in 3-dimensional space with a plane
    a. Cross section0
    b. Thing
    c. Undefined
    d. Undefined

120. In mathematics, _____ geometry was the traditional name for the geometry of three-dimensional Euclidean space — for practical purposes the kind of space we live in.
    a. Solid0
    b. Thing
    c. Undefined
    d. Undefined

121. A _____ surface is the surface or face of a solid on its sides. It can also be defined as any face or surface that is not a base.
    a. Lateral0
    b. Thing
    c. Undefined
    d. Undefined

Chapter 7. Integrals Over Paths and Surfaces

122. _____ of Syracuse was an ancient Greek mathematician, physicist and engineer. In addition to making important discoveries in the field of mathematics and geometry, he is credited with producing machines that were well ahead of their time.
    a. Archimedes0
    b. Person
    c. Undefined
    d. Undefined

123. _____ is the design, analysis, and/or construction of works for practical purposes.
    a. Thing
    b. Engineering0
    c. Undefined
    d. Undefined

124. In Euclidean geometry, a uniform _____ is a linear transformation that enlargers or diminishes objects, and whose _____ factor is the same in all directions. This is also called homothethy.
    a. Scale0
    b. Thing
    c. Undefined
    d. Undefined

125. _____ numerals are a numeral system originating in ancient Rome, adapted from Etruscan numerals.
    a. Thing
    b. Roman0
    c. Undefined
    d. Undefined

126. A _____ is a quantity that denotes the proportional amount or magnitude of one quantity relative to another.
    a. Ratio0
    b. Thing
    c. Undefined
    d. Undefined

127. A _____ is a deliberate process for transforming one or more inputs into one or more results.
    a. Thing
    b. Calculation0
    c. Undefined
    d. Undefined

128. In mathematics, a _____ is a countable collection of open covers of a topological space that satisfies certain separation axioms.
    a. Thing
    b. Development0
    c. Undefined
    d. Undefined

129. _____ is a quadric
    a. Thing
    b. Paraboloid0
    c. Undefined
    d. Undefined

130. Leonhard _____ was a pioneering Swiss mathematician and physicist, who spent most of his life in Russia and Germany.
    a. Person
    b. Euler0
    c. Undefined
    d. Undefined

131. _____ was a pioneering Swiss mathematician and physicist, who spent most of his life in Russia and Germany.
    a. Leonhard Euler0
    b. Person
    c. Undefined
    d. Undefined

Chapter 7. Integrals Over Paths and Surfaces

132. _____ is a reaction force applied by a stretched string on the objects which stretch it.
   a. Thing
   b. Tension0
   c. Undefined
   d. Undefined

133. _____, FRS was an English chemist and physicist who contributed significantly to the fields of electromagnetism and electrochemistry
   a. Person
   b. Michael Faraday0
   c. Undefined
   d. Undefined

134. A _____ is a mathematical equation for an unknown function of one or several variables which relates the values of the function itself and of its derivatives of various orders.
   a. Differential equation0
   b. Thing
   c. Undefined
   d. Undefined

135. In geometry, a _____ is defined as a quadrilateral where all four of its angles are right angles.
   a. Thing
   b. Rectangle0
   c. Undefined
   d. Undefined

136. The _____ of a right circular cone is the distance from any point on the circle to the apex of the cone.
   a. Thing
   b. Slant height0
   c. Undefined
   d. Undefined

137. _____ is either of the two parts into which a plane divides the three-dimensional space. More generally, a _____ is either of the two parts into which a hyperplane divides an affine space.
   a. Thing
   b. Half-space0
   c. Undefined
   d. Undefined

138. A _____ is one of the basic shapes of geometry: a polygon with three vertices and three sides which are straight line segments.
   a. Triangle0
   b. Thing
   c. Undefined
   d. Undefined

139. An _____ is the limit of a definite integral, as an endpoint of the interval of integration approaches either a specified real number or ‡ or − ‡ or, in some cases, as both endpoints approach limits.
   a. Improper integral0
   b. Thing
   c. Undefined
   d. Undefined

140. In mathematics, an _____ is a statement about the relative size or order of two objects.
   a. Inequality0
   b. Thing
   c. Undefined
   d. Undefined

141. A _____ (plural: tetrahedra) is a polyhedron composed of four triangular faces, three of which meet at each vertex.
   a. Tetrahedron0
   b. Thing
   c. Undefined
   d. Undefined

Chapter 7. Integrals Over Paths and Surfaces

142. A _____ is a three-dimensional solid object bounded by six square faces, facets, or sides, with three meeting at each vertex.
   a. Cube0
   b. Thing
   c. Undefined
   d. Undefined

143. Two mathematical objects are equal if and only if they are precisely the same in every way. This defines a binary relation, _____, denoted by the sign of _____ "=" in such a way that the statement "x = y" means that x and y are equal.
   a. Equality0
   b. Thing
   c. Undefined
   d. Undefined

144. In mathematics, the term _____ is applied to certain functions. There are two common ways it is applied: these are related historically, but diverged somewhat during the twentieth century.
   a. Functional0
   b. Thing
   c. Undefined
   d. Undefined

145. In mathematical analysis, a _____ is a classification of functions according to the properties of their derivatives.
   a. Smooth surface0
   b. Thing
   c. Undefined
   d. Undefined

146. In mathematics, a _____ is a demonstration that, assuming certain axioms, some statement is necessarily true.
   a. Proof0
   b. Thing
   c. Undefined
   d. Undefined

147. In acoustics and telecommunication, the _____ of a wave is a component frequency of the signal that is an integer multiple of the fundamental frequency.
   a. Thing
   b. Harmonic0
   c. Undefined
   d. Undefined

148. An _____ is one of eight divisions.
   a. Thing
   b. Octant0
   c. Undefined
   d. Undefined

149. _____ of an object is its speed in a particular direction.
   a. Thing
   b. Velocity0
   c. Undefined
   d. Undefined

150. _____ is bother the congnitive process of transferring information from a particular subject , and a linguistic expression corresponding to such a process.
   a. Thing
   b. Analogy0
   c. Undefined
   d. Undefined

151. A _____ is a function for which, intuitively, small changes in the input result in small changes in the output.

a. Event
b. Continuous function0
c. Undefined
d. Undefined

152. In mathematics and applications, given a vector to a surface at a point, that vector can be decomposed uniquely as a sum of two vectors, one tangent to the surface, called the tangential component of the vector, and another one perpendicular to the surface, called the _____ of the vector.
a. Thing
b. Normal component0
c. Undefined
d. Undefined

153. Generally, a _____ is a splitting of something into parts.
a. Thing
b. Partition0
c. Undefined
d. Undefined

154. In fluid dynamics the flow velocity, or _____, of a fluid is a vector field which is used to mathematically describe the motion of the fluid.
a. Thing
b. Velocity field0
c. Undefined
d. Undefined

155. A _____ is a four-sided plane figure that has two sets of opposite parallel sides.
a. Concept
b. Parallelogram0
c. Undefined
d. Undefined

156. A _____ is a function that assigns a number to subsets of a given set.
a. Measure0
b. Thing
c. Undefined
d. Undefined

157. _____ is a kind of property which exists as magnitude or multitude. It is among the basic classes of things along with quality, substance, change, and relation.
a. Amount0
b. Thing
c. Undefined
d. Undefined

158. In topology and related areas of mathematics a _____ or Moore-Smith sequence is a generalization of a sequence, intended to unify the various notions of limit and generalize them to arbitrary topological spaces.
a. Thing
b. Net0
c. Undefined
d. Undefined

159. In the field of electromagnetism, _____ is usually the integral of a vector quantity over a finite surface.
a. Thing
b. Flux0
c. Undefined
d. Undefined

160. An _____ or member of a set is an object that when collected together make up the set.
a. Element0
b. Thing
c. Undefined
d. Undefined

161. The metre (or _____, see spelling differences) is a measure of length. It is the basic unit of length in the metric system and in the International System of Units (SI), used around the world for general and scientific purposes.

Chapter 7. Integrals Over Paths and Surfaces

a. Concept
b. Meter0
c. Undefined
d. Undefined

162. A _____ is a set whose members are members of another set or a set contained within another set.
a. Subset0
b. Thing
c. Undefined
d. Undefined

163. An _____ is a type of quadric surface that is a higher dimensional analogue of an ellipse.
a. Thing
b. Ellipsoid0
c. Undefined
d. Undefined

164. _____ was a German mathematician and scientist of profound genius who contributed significantly to many fields, including number theory, analysis, differential geometry, geodesy, magnetism, astronomy, and optics.
a. Person
b. Karl Friedrich Gauss0
c. Undefined
d. Undefined

165. _____, Greek for "knowledge of nature," is the branch of science concerned with the discovery and characterization of universal laws which govern matter, energy, space, and time.
a. Thing
b. Physics0
c. Undefined
d. Undefined

166. Sir _____ was an English physicist, mathematician, astronomer, natural philosopher, and alchemist, regarded by many as the greatest figure in the history of science.
a. Isaac Newton0
b. Person
c. Undefined
d. Undefined

167. _____ is defined as the rate of change or derivative with respect to time of velocity.
a. Thing
b. Acceleration0
c. Undefined
d. Undefined

168. In mathematical analysis and related areas of mathematics, a set is called _____, if it is, in a certain sense, of finite size.
a. Bounded0
b. Thing
c. Undefined
d. Undefined

169. In mathematics, a class _____ is a structure used to organize the various Galois groups and modules that appear in class field theory. They were invented by Emil Artin and John Tate.
a. Thing
b. Formation0
c. Undefined
d. Undefined

170. _____ are external two-dimensional outlines, with the appearance or configuration of some thing - in contrast to the matter or content or substance of which it is composed.
a. Shapes0
b. Thing
c. Undefined
d. Undefined

Chapter 7. Integrals Over Paths and Surfaces

171. In mathematics, the word _____ is used informally to refer to certain distinct bodies of knowledge about mathematics.
   a. Thing
   b. Theoretical0
   c. Undefined
   d. Undefined

172. The _____ is defined as the summation of all particles and energy that exist and the space-time which all events occur.
   a. Thing
   b. Universe0
   c. Undefined
   d. Undefined

173. An _____ of a product of sums expresses it as a sum of products by using the fact that multiplication distributes over addition.
   a. Expansion0
   b. Thing
   c. Undefined
   d. Undefined

174. _____ is electromagnetic radiation with a wavelength that is visible to the eye (visible _____) or, in a technical or scientific context, electromagnetic radiation of any wavelength.
   a. Thing
   b. Light0
   c. Undefined
   d. Undefined

175. _____ is the weakest of the four fundamental forces of bature, as described by Issac Newton
   a. Thing
   b. Gravitational force0
   c. Undefined
   d. Undefined

176. A _____ is a unit of length, usually used to measure distance, in a number of different systems, including Imperial units, United States customary units and Norwegian/Swedish mil. Its size can vary from system to system, but in each is between 1 and 10 kilometers. In contemporary English contexts _____ refers to either:
   a. Mile0
   b. Thing
   c. Undefined
   d. Undefined

177. _____ (March 14, 1879 - April 18, 1955) was a German-born theoretical physicist who is best known for his theory of relativity and specifically mass-energy equivalence, $E = mc^2$.
   a. Person
   b. Albert Einstein0
   c. Undefined
   d. Undefined

178. _____ is the transport of people on a trip/journey or the process or time involved in a person or object moving from one location to another.
   a. Travel0
   b. Thing
   c. Undefined
   d. Undefined

179. _____ is the path a moving object follows through space.
   a. Thing
   b. Projectile motion0
   c. Undefined
   d. Undefined

180. In physics, an _____ is the path that an object makes around another object while under the influence of a source of centripetal force, such as gravity.

a. Thing
c. Undefined

b. Orbit0
d. Undefined

181. In mathematics, an _____ is something that does not change under a set of transformations. The property of being an _____ is invariance.
a. Thing
c. Undefined

b. Invariant0
d. Undefined

182. In mathematics, a _____ is an algebraic structure in which addition and multiplication are defined and have properties listed below.
a. Ring0
c. Undefined

b. Thing
d. Undefined

183. In statistics, a _____ measure is one which is measuring what is supposed to measure.
a. Thing
c. Undefined

b. Valid0
d. Undefined

Chapter 8. The Integral Theorems of Vector Analysis

1. In physics and in _____ calculus, a spatial _____, or simply _____, is a concept characterized by a magnitude and a direction.
   a. Vector0
   b. Thing
   c. Undefined
   d. Undefined

2. In mathematics, the _____ of a coordinate system is the point where the axes of the system intersect.
   a. Origin0
   b. Thing
   c. Undefined
   d. Undefined

3. The _____ of a function is an extension of the concept of a sum, and are identified or found through the use of integration.
   a. Thing
   b. Integral0
   c. Undefined
   d. Undefined

4. In mathematics, a _____ is a statement that can be proved on the basis of explicitly stated or previously agreed assumptions.
   a. Thing
   b. Theorem0
   c. Undefined
   d. Undefined

5. In mathematics, an _____ on a real vector space is a choice of which ordered bases are "positively" oriented, or right-handed, and which are "negatively" oriented, or left-handed.
   a. Orientation0
   b. Thing
   c. Undefined
   d. Undefined

6. In mathematics and the mathematical sciences, a _____ is a fixed, but possibly unspecified, value. This is in contrast to a variable, which is not fixed.
   a. Constant0
   b. Thing
   c. Undefined
   d. Undefined

7. In mathematics, a _____ is a two-dimensional manifold or surface that is perfectly flat.
   a. Thing
   b. Plane0
   c. Undefined
   d. Undefined

8. In mathematics, the concept of a _____ tries to capture the intuitive idea of a geometrical one-dimensional and continuous object. A simple example is the circle.
   a. Curve0
   b. Thing
   c. Undefined
   d. Undefined

9. _____ is a mathematical subject that includes the study of limits, derivatives, integrals, and power series and constitutes a major part of modern university curriculum.
   a. Thing
   b. Calculus0
   c. Undefined
   d. Undefined

10. In number theory, the _____ of arithmetic (or unique factorization theorem) states that every natural number greater than 1 can be written as a unique product of prime numbers.

Chapter 8. The Integral Theorems of Vector Analysis

    a. Concept
    c. Undefined
    b. Fundamental theorem0
    d. Undefined

11. _____ of calculus is the statement that the two central operations of calculus, differentiation and integration, are inverse operations: if a continuous function is first integrated and then differentiated, the original function is retrieved.
    a. Fundamental Theorem of Calculus0
    b. Thing
    c. Undefined
    d. Undefined

12. Two mathematical objects are equal if and only if they are precisely the same in every way. This defines a binary relation, _____, denoted by the sign of _____ "=" in such a way that the statement "x = y" means that x and y are equal.
    a. Thing
    b. Equality0
    c. Undefined
    d. Undefined

13. In mathematics, the additive inverse, or _____ of a number n is the number that, when added to n, yields zero. The additive inverse of n is denoted −n. For example, 7 is −7, because 7 + (−7) = 0, and the additive inverse of −0.3 is 0.3, because −0.3 + 0.3 = 0.
    a. Thing
    b. Opposite0
    c. Undefined
    d. Undefined

14. In mathematics, the _____ of a number n is the number that, when added to n, yields zero. The _____ of n is denoted −n. For example, 7 is −7, because 7 + (−7) = 0, and the _____ of −0.3 is 0.3, because −0.3 + 0.3 = 0.
    a. Thing
    b. Additive inverse0
    c. Undefined
    d. Undefined

15. In mathematics, a _____ sometimes called a path integral is an integral where the function to be integrated is evaluated along a curve
    a. Thing
    b. Line integral0
    c. Undefined
    d. Undefined

16. _____ is a circle with a unit radius, i.e., a circle whose radius is 1.
    a. Unit circle0
    b. Thing
    c. Undefined
    d. Undefined

17. In Euclidean geometry, a _____ is the set of all points in a plane at a fixed distance, called the radius, from a given point, the center.
    a. Circle0
    b. Thing
    c. Undefined
    d. Undefined

18. _____ means "constancy", i.e. if something retains a certain feature even after we change a way of looking at it, then it is symmetric.
    a. Thing
    b. Symmetry0
    c. Undefined
    d. Undefined

19. In mathematics, a _____ is a connected curve that does not intersect itself and ends at the same point in which it starts.

Chapter 8. The Integral Theorems of Vector Analysis

    a. Thing
    c. Undefined
    b. Closed curve0
    d. Undefined

20. In mathematical analysis and related areas of mathematics, a set is called _____, if it is, in a certain sense, of finite size.
    a. Bounded0
    b. Thing
    c. Undefined
    d. Undefined

21. In mathematics, a _____ is a demonstration that, assuming certain axioms, some statement is necessarily true.
    a. Proof0
    b. Thing
    c. Undefined
    d. Undefined

22. In mathematics, the _____ functions are functions of an angle; they are important when studying triangles and modeling periodic phenomena, among many other applications.
    a. Thing
    b. Trigonometric0
    c. Undefined
    d. Undefined

23. An _____ is an equality that remains true regardless of the values of any variables that appear within it, to distinguish it from an equality which is true under more particular conditions.
    a. Thing
    b. Identity0
    c. Undefined
    d. Undefined

24. _____ is a construction in vector calculus which associates a vector to every point in a locally Euclidean space.
    a. Thing
    b. Vector field0
    c. Undefined
    d. Undefined

25. In common philosophical language, a proposition or _____, is the content of an assertion, that is, it is true-or-false and defined by the meaning of a particular piece of language.
    a. Concept
    b. Statement0
    c. Undefined
    d. Undefined

26. _____ is an operator that measures the magnitude of a vector field's source or sink at a given point; the _____ of a vector field is a signed scalar.
    a. Divergence0
    b. Thing
    c. Undefined
    d. Undefined

27. In vector calculus, the _____ is a result that relates the flow, or flux, of a vector field through a surface to the behavior of the vector field inside the surface.
    a. Thing
    b. Divergence theorem0
    c. Undefined
    d. Undefined

28. In trigonometry, the _____ is a function defined as $\tan x = \sin x / \cos x$. The function is so-named because it can be defined as the length of a certain segment of a _____ (in the geometric sense) to the unit circle. In plane geometry, a line is _____ to a curve, at some point, if both line and curve pass through the point with the same direction.

a. Tangent0
b. Thing
c. Undefined
d. Undefined

29. In mathematics and applications, given a vector to a surface at a point, that vector can be decomposed uniquely as a sum of two vectors, one tangent to the surface, called the tangential component of the vector, and another one perpendicular to the surface, called the _____ of the vector.
   a. Thing
   b. Normal component0
   c. Undefined
   d. Undefined

30. In plane geometry, a _____ is a polygon with four equal sides, four right angles, and parallel opposite sides. In algebra, the _____ of a number is that number multiplied by itself.
   a. Thing
   b. Square0
   c. Undefined
   d. Undefined

31. In mathematics, in the field of group theory, a _____ of a group is a quasisimple subnormal subgroup.
   a. Component0
   b. Concept
   c. Undefined
   d. Undefined

32. In classical geometry, a _____ of a circle or sphere is any line segment from its center to its boundary. By extension, the _____ of a circle or sphere is the length of any such segment. The _____ is half the diameter. In science and engineering the term _____ of curvature is commonly used as a synonym for _____.
   a. Thing
   b. Radius0
   c. Undefined
   d. Undefined

33. In geometry, the _____ of an object is a point in some sense in the middle of the object.
   a. Thing
   b. Center0
   c. Undefined
   d. Undefined

34. The mathematical concept of a _____ expresses the intuitive idea of deterministic dependence between two quantities, one of which is viewed as primary and the other as secondary. A _____ then is a way to associate a unique output for each input of a specified type, for example, a real number or an element of a given set.
   a. Thing
   b. Function0
   c. Undefined
   d. Undefined

35. In Euclidean geometry, an _____ is a closed segment of a differentiable curve in the two-dimensional plane; for example, a circular _____ is a segment of a circle.
   a. Arc0
   b. Concept
   c. Undefined
   d. Undefined

36. A _____ is the curve defined by the path of a point on the edge of circular wheel as the wheel rolls along a straight line.
   a. Cycloid0
   b. Thing
   c. Undefined
   d. Undefined

37. An _____ is a straight line around which a geometric figure can be rotated.

Chapter 8. The Integral Theorems of Vector Analysis

a. Axis0
b. Thing
c. Undefined
d. Undefined

38. A _____ is a set of numbers that designate location in a given reference system, such as x,y in a planar _____ system or an x,y,z in a three-dimensional _____ system.
   a. Coordinate0
   b. Thing
   c. Undefined
   d. Undefined

39. In mathematics, an _____ .
   a. Thing
   b. Ellipse0
   c. Undefined
   d. Undefined

40. In functional analysis and related areas of mathematics the _____ set of a given subset of a vector space is a certain set in the dual space.
   a. Thing
   b. Polar0
   c. Undefined
   d. Undefined

41. In mathematics, a _____ or rhodonea curve is a sinusoid plotted in polar coordinates.
   a. Thing
   b. Rose0
   c. Undefined
   d. Undefined

42. A _____ is traditionally an infinitesimally small change in a variable.
   a. Thing
   b. Differential0
   c. Undefined
   d. Undefined

43. A _____ is a mathematical equation for an unknown function of one or several variables which relates the values of the function itself and of its derivatives of various orders.
   a. Differential equation0
   b. Thing
   c. Undefined
   d. Undefined

44. In acoustics and telecommunication, the _____ of a wave is a component frequency of the signal that is an integer multiple of the fundamental frequency.
   a. Harmonic0
   b. Thing
   c. Undefined
   d. Undefined

45. A _____ signifies a point or points of probability on a subject e.g., the _____ of creativity, which allows for the formation of rule or norm or law by interpretation of the phenomena events that can be created.
   a. Principle0
   b. Thing
   c. Undefined
   d. Undefined

46. In statistics, a _____ measure is one which is measuring what is supposed to measure.
   a. Valid0
   b. Thing
   c. Undefined
   d. Undefined

47. In mathematics and applications, given a vector to a surface at a point, that vector can be decomposed uniquely as a sum of two vectors, one tangent to the surface, called the _____ of the vector.

Chapter 8. The Integral Theorems of Vector Analysis

a. Tangential component0
b. Thing
c. Undefined
d. Undefined

48. In calculus, the _____ is a formula for the derivative of the composite of two functions.
a. Concept
b. Chain rule0
c. Undefined
d. Undefined

49. An _____ is a combination of numbers, operators, grouping symbols and/or free variables and bound variables arranged in a meaningful way which can be evaluated..
a. Expression0
b. Thing
c. Undefined
d. Undefined

50. In mathematics, the _____ f is the collection of all ordered pairs . In particular, graph means the graphical representation of this collection, in the form of a curve or surface, together with axes, etc. Graphing on a Cartesian plane is sometimes referred to as curve sketching.
a. Thing
b. Graph of a function0
c. Undefined
d. Undefined

51. In mathematics, a _____ is a quadric surface, with the following equation in Cartesian coordinates: $(x/a)^2 + (y/b)^2 = 1$.
a. Thing
b. Cylinder0
c. Undefined
d. Undefined

52. In mathematics, the _____ of two sets A and B is the set that contains all elements of A that also belong to B (or equivalently, all elements of B that also belong to A), but no other elements.
a. Intersection0
b. Thing
c. Undefined
d. Undefined

53. _____ is a function that extends the concept of an ordinary sum
a. Thing
b. Integrand0
c. Undefined
d. Undefined

54. In mathematics, a _____ is the set of all points in three-dimensional space (R^3) which are at distance r from a fixed point of that space, where r is a positive real number called the radius of the _____. The fixed point is called the center or centre, and is not part of the _____ itself.
a. Sphere0
b. Thing
c. Undefined
d. Undefined

55. In geometry, two lines or planes if one falls on the other in such a way as to create congruent adjacent angles. The term may be used as a noun or adjective. Thus, referring to Figure 1, the line AB is the _____ to CD through the point B.
a. Thing
b. Perpendicular0
c. Undefined
d. Undefined

56. The _____, the average in everyday English, which is also called the arithmetic _____ (and is distinguished from the geometric _____ or harmonic _____). The average is also called the sample _____. The expected value of a random variable, which is also called the population _____.

a. Mean0 b. Thing
c. Undefined d. Undefined

57. In topology and related areas of mathematics a _____ or Moore-Smith sequence is a generalization of a sequence, intended to unify the various notions of limit and generalize them to arbitrary topological spaces.
a. Net0 b. Thing
c. Undefined d. Undefined

58. _____ is a kind of property which exists as magnitude or multitude. It is among the basic classes of things along with quality, substance, change, and relation.
a. Thing b. Amount0
c. Undefined d. Undefined

59. _____ of an object is its speed in a particular direction.
a. Velocity0 b. Thing
c. Undefined d. Undefined

60. In fluid dynamics the flow velocity, or _____, of a fluid is a vector field which is used to mathematically describe the motion of the fluid.
a. Velocity field0 b. Thing
c. Undefined d. Undefined

61. In mathematics, a _____ is the result of multiplying, or an expression that identifies factors to be multiplied.
a. Product0 b. Thing
c. Undefined d. Undefined

62. _____ in a normed vector space is a vector whose length, or magnitude is 1.
a. Unit vector0 b. Thing
c. Undefined d. Undefined

63. In mathematics, the _____, also known as the scalar product, is a binary operation which takes two vectors over the real numbers R and returns a real-valued scalar quantity. It is the standard inner product of the Euclidean space.
a. Dot product0 b. Thing
c. Undefined d. Undefined

64. The _____ of a mathematical object is its size: a property by which it can be larger or smaller than other objects of the same kind; in technical terms, an ordering of the class of objects to which it belongs.
a. Thing b. Magnitude0
c. Undefined d. Undefined

65. In linear algebra, two vectors in an inner product space are _____ if they are orthogonal (their inner product is 0) and both of unit length (the norm of each is 1). A set of vectors which is pairwise _____ (any two vectors in it are _____) is called an _____ set. A basis which forms an _____ set is called an _____ basis.
a. Orthonormal0 b. Thing
c. Undefined d. Undefined

Chapter 8. The Integral Theorems of Vector Analysis

66. In mathematics and its applications, a _____ is a system for assigning an n-tuple of numbers or scalars to each point in an n-dimensional space.
   a. Coordinate system0
   b. Concept
   c. Undefined
   d. Undefined

67. In mathematics and its applications, _____ are used for assigning an n-tuple of numbers or scalars to each point in an n-dimensional space.
   a. Coordinate systems0
   b. Concept
   c. Undefined
   d. Undefined

68. In vector calculus, the _____ of a scalar field is a vector field which points in the direction of the greatest rate of increase of the scalar field, and whose magnitude is the greatest rate of change.
   a. Gradient0
   b. Thing
   c. Undefined
   d. Undefined

69. In mathematics, science including computer science, linguistics and engineering, an _____ is, generally speaking, an independent variable or input to a function.
   a. Argument0
   b. Thing
   c. Undefined
   d. Undefined

70. The deductive-nomological model is a formalized view of scientific _____ in natural language.
   a. Explanation0
   b. Thing
   c. Undefined
   d. Undefined

71. Deductive _____ is the kind of _____ in which the conclusion is necessitated by, or reached from, previously known facts (the premises).
   a. Reasoning0
   b. Thing
   c. Undefined
   d. Undefined

72. In mathematics, _____ refers to a number of loosely related concepts in different areas of geometry. Intuitively, _____ is the amount by which a geometric object deviates from being flat, but this is defined in different ways depending on the context
   a. Curvature0
   b. Thing
   c. Undefined
   d. Undefined

73. In astronomy, geography, geometry and related sciences and contexts, a plane is said to be _____ at a given point if it is locally perpendicular to the gradient of the gravity field, i.e., with the direction of the gravitational force at that point.
   a. Thing
   b. Horizontal0
   c. Undefined
   d. Undefined

74. In mathematics, two quantities are called _____ if they vary in such a way that one of the quantities is a constant multiple of the other, or equivalently if they have a constant ratio.
   a. Proportional0
   b. Thing
   c. Undefined
   d. Undefined

75. In physics, the _____ momentum of an object rotating about some reference point is the measure of the extent to which the object will continue to rotate about that point unless acted upon by an external torque.
- a. Thing
- b. Angular0
- c. Undefined
- d. Undefined

76. A _____ is a special kind of ratio, indicating a relationship between two measurements with different units, such as miles to gallons or cents to pounds.
- a. Rate0
- b. Thing
- c. Undefined
- d. Undefined

77. In physics, the _____ is a vector quantity (more precisely, a pseudovector) which specifies the angular speed at which an object is rotating along with the direction in which it is rotating.
- a. Angular velocity0
- b. Thing
- c. Undefined
- d. Undefined

78. A _____ is one of the basic shapes of geometry: a polygon with three vertices and three sides which are straight line segments.
- a. Triangle0
- b. Thing
- c. Undefined
- d. Undefined

79. A _____ is a movement of an object in a circular motion. A two-dimensional object rotates around a center (or point) of _____. A three-dimensional object rotates around a line called an axis. If the axis of _____ is within the body, the body is said to rotate upon itself, or spin—which implies relative speed and perhaps free-movement with angular momentum. A circular motion about an external point, e.g. the Earth about the Sun, is called an orbit or more properly an orbital revolution.
- a. Thing
- b. Rotation0
- c. Undefined
- d. Undefined

80. _____ is a circle on the surface of a sphere that has the same circumference as the sphere, dividing the sphere into two equal hemispheres.
- a. Thing
- b. Great circle0
- c. Undefined
- d. Undefined

81. In linear algebra and geometry, a rotation (_____) is a type of transformation from one system of coordinates to another system of coordinates such that distance between any two points remains invariant under the transformation.
- a. Thing
- b. Rotational0
- c. Undefined
- d. Undefined

82. In set theory and other branches of mathematics, the _____ of a collection of sets is the set that contains everything that belongs to any of the sets, but nothing else.
- a. Union0
- b. Thing
- c. Undefined
- d. Undefined

83. A _____ is a deliberate process for transforming one or more inputs into one or more results.

Chapter 8. The Integral Theorems of Vector Analysis

    a. Thing
    b. Calculation0
    c. Undefined
    d. Undefined

84. An _____ is a type of quadric surface that is a higher dimensional analogue of an ellipse.
    a. Ellipsoid0
    b. Thing
    c. Undefined
    d. Undefined

85. The _____ of a solid object is the three-dimensional concept of how much space it occupies, often quantified numerically.
    a. Thing
    b. Volume0
    c. Undefined
    d. Undefined

86. _____ after the plane and the catenoid, is the third minimal surface to be known.
    a. Helicoid0
    b. Thing
    c. Undefined
    d. Undefined

87. In the field of electromagnetism, _____ is usually the integral of a vector quantity over a finite surface.
    a. Thing
    b. Flux0
    c. Undefined
    d. Undefined

88. In financial mathematics, the _____ volatility of an option contract is the volatility _____ by the market price of the option based on an option pricing model.
    a. Implied0
    b. Thing
    c. Undefined
    d. Undefined

89. _____ is mass m per unit volume V.
    a. Density0
    b. Thing
    c. Undefined
    d. Undefined

90. In geometry, an _____ is a point at which a line segment or ray terminates.
    a. Thing
    b. Endpoint0
    c. Undefined
    d. Undefined

91. In vector calculus a _____ is a vector field which is the gradient of a scalar potential.
    a. Conservative field0
    b. Thing
    c. Undefined
    d. Undefined

92. In physics, _____ is an influence that may cause an object to accelerate. It may be experienced as a lift, a push, or a pull. The actual acceleration of the body is determined by the vector sum of all forces acting on it, known as net _____ or resultant _____.
    a. Force0
    b. Thing
    c. Undefined
    d. Undefined

93. In mathematics, a set is called _____ if there is a bijection between the set and some set of the form {1, 2, ..., n} where n is a natural number.

Chapter 8. The Integral Theorems of Vector Analysis

a. Finite0
b. Thing
c. Undefined
d. Undefined

94. A _____ function curves downwards. The graph of a _____ function of one variable remains above its tangents and below its cords.
    a. Convex0
    b. Thing
    c. Undefined
    d. Undefined

95. In mathematics, _____ are the intuitive idea of a geometrical one-dimensional and continuous object.
    a. Thing
    b. Curves0
    c. Undefined
    d. Undefined

96. The _____ is a unit of plane angle, equivalent to $1/400$ of a full circle, dividing a right angle in 100.
    a. Grad0
    b. Thing
    c. Undefined
    d. Undefined

97. A _____ consists either of a suggested explanation for a phenomenon or of a reasoned proposal suggesting a possible correlation between multiple phenomena.
    a. Hypothesis0
    b. Thing
    c. Undefined
    d. Undefined

98. _____ is a set, with some particular properties and usually some additional structure, such as the operations of addition or multiplication, for instance.
    a. Space0
    b. Thing
    c. Undefined
    d. Undefined

99. _____ is a vector field whose curl is zero.
    a. Thing
    b. Conservative vector field0
    c. Undefined
    d. Undefined

100. In linear algebra, real numbers are called scalars and relate to vectors in a vector space through the operation of _____ multiplication, in which a vector can be multiplied by a number to produce another vector.
     a. Thing
     b. Scalar0
     c. Undefined
     d. Undefined

101. In physics, a _____ may refer to the scalar _____ or to the vector _____.
     a. Potential0
     b. Thing
     c. Undefined
     d. Undefined

102. _____ is the property of a physical object that quantifies the amount of matter and energy it is equivalent to.
     a. Thing
     b. Mass0
     c. Undefined
     d. Undefined

103. A _____ is a mathematical statement which follows easily from a previously proven statement, typically a mathematical theorem.

Chapter 8. The Integral Theorems of Vector Analysis

a. Thing
b. Corollary0
c. Undefined
d. Undefined

104. A _____ defined function f(x) of a real variable x is a function whose definition is given differently on disjoint subsets of its domain.
a. Thing
b. Piecewise0
c. Undefined
d. Undefined

105. _____ is the path a moving object follows through space.
a. Projectile motion0
b. Thing
c. Undefined
d. Undefined

106. _____ is the weakest of the four fundamental forces of bature, as described by Issac Newton
a. Gravitational force0
b. Thing
c. Undefined
d. Undefined

107. In mathematics, _____ geometry was the traditional name for the geometry of three-dimensional Euclidean space — for practical purposes the kind of space we live in.
a. Solid0
b. Thing
c. Undefined
d. Undefined

108. In topology, the _____ are subsets S of a topological space X is the set of points which can be approached both from S and from the outside of S.
a. Thing
b. Boundaries0
c. Undefined
d. Undefined

109. In mathematics, _____ refers to the rewriting of an expression into a simpler form.
a. Reduction0
b. Thing
c. Undefined
d. Undefined

110. In mathematics, a _____ of a k-place relation $L \subseteq X_1 \times ... \times X_k$ is one of the sets X_j, $1 \leq j \leq k$. In the special case where k = 2 and $L \subseteq X_1 \times X_2$ is a function $L : X_1 \to X_2$, it is conventional to refer to X_1 as the _____ of the function and to refer to X_2 as the codomain of the function.
a. Thing
b. Domain0
c. Undefined
d. Undefined

111. _____ are the basic objects of study in graph theory. Informally speaking, a graph is a set of objects called points, nodes, or vertices connected by links called lines or edges.
a. Thing
b. Graphs0
c. Undefined
d. Undefined

112. In mathematics and logic, a _____ proof is a way of showing the truth or falsehood of a given statement by a straightforward combination of established facts, usually existing lemmas and theorems, without making any further assumptions.

Chapter 8. The Integral Theorems of Vector Analysis

    a. Thing
    c. Undefined
    b. Direct0
    d. Undefined

113. In mathematics, _____ are two-dimensional manifolds or surfaces that are perfectly flat.
    a. Planes0
    c. Undefined
    b. Thing
    d. Undefined

114. A _____ is a symbolic representation denoting a quantity or expression. It often represents an "unknown" quantity that has the potential to change.
    a. Thing
    c. Undefined
    b. Variable0
    d. Undefined

115. In mathematics, _____ is synonymous with perpendicular when used as a simple adjective that is not part of any longer phrase with a standard definition. It means at right angles. It comes from the Greek ἀντί ὀρθός, orthos, meaning "straight", used by Euclid to mean right; and γωνία gonia, meaning angle. Two streets that cross each other at a right angle are _____ to one another.
    a. Orthogonal0
    c. Undefined
    b. Thing
    d. Undefined

116. A _____ is a negotiable instrument instructing a financial institution to pay a specific amount of a specific currency from a specific demand account held in the maker/depositor's name with that institution. Both the maker and payee may be natural persons or legal entities.
    a. Check0
    c. Undefined
    b. Thing
    d. Undefined

117. A _____ is a three-dimensional solid object bounded by six square faces, facets, or sides, with three meeting at each vertex.
    a. Thing
    c. Undefined
    b. Cube0
    d. Undefined

118. An _____ is one of eight divisions.
    a. Octant0
    c. Undefined
    b. Thing
    d. Undefined

119. Sir Isaac _____, was an English physicist, mathematician, astronomer, natural philosopher, and alchemist, regarded by many as the greatest figure in the history of science
    a. Newton0
    c. Undefined
    b. Person
    d. Undefined

120. Sir _____ was an English physicist, mathematician, astronomer, natural philosopher, and alchemist, regarded by many as the greatest figure in the history of science.
    a. Person
    c. Undefined
    b. Isaac Newton0
    d. Undefined

121. Equivalence is the condition of being _____ or essentially equal.

Chapter 8. The Integral Theorems of Vector Analysis

    a. Equivalent0
    c. Undefined
    b. Thing
    d. Undefined

122. In mathematics and physics, a _____ associates a scalar value, which can be either mathematical in definition, or physical, to every point in space.
    a. Thing
    c. Undefined
    b. Scalar field0
    d. Undefined

123. In mathematics, _____ is a part of the set theoretic notion of function.
    a. Image0
    c. Undefined
    b. Thing
    d. Undefined

124. Leonhard _____ was a pioneering Swiss mathematician and physicist, who spent most of his life in Russia and Germany.
    a. Euler0
    c. Undefined
    b. Person
    d. Undefined

125. _____ was a pioneering Swiss mathematician and physicist, who spent most of his life in Russia and Germany.
    a. Leonhard Euler0
    c. Undefined
    b. Person
    d. Undefined

126. _____ is a physical property of a system that underlies the common notions of hot and cold; something that is hotter has the greater _____.
    a. Thing
    c. Undefined
    b. Temperature0
    d. Undefined

127. The plus and _____ signs are mathematical symbols used to represent the notions of positive and negative as well as the operations of addition and subtraction.
    a. Minus0
    c. Undefined
    b. Thing
    d. Undefined

128. Initial objects are also called _____, and terminal objects are also called final.
    a. Coterminal0
    c. Undefined
    b. Thing
    d. Undefined

129. In mathematics, in the field of differential equations, an initial value problem is a differential equation together with specified value, called the _____, of the unknown function at a given point in the domain of the solution.
    a. Initial condition0
    c. Undefined
    b. Thing
    d. Undefined

130. A _____ is a statement or claimt that a particular event will occur in the future in more certain terms than a forecast.
    a. Prediction0
    c. Undefined
    b. Thing
    d. Undefined

Chapter 8. The Integral Theorems of Vector Analysis

131. In mathematical analysis, _____ are objects which generalize functions and probability distributions.
   a. Thing
   b. Distribution0
   c. Undefined
   d. Undefined

132. The _____ of measurement are a globally standardized and modernized form of the metric system.
   a. Units0
   b. Thing
   c. Undefined
   d. Undefined

133. In mathematics, factorization (British English: factorisation) or factoring is the decomposition of an object (for example, a number, a polynomial, or a matrix) into a product of other objects, or _____, which when multiplied together give the original.
   a. Factors0
   b. Thing
   c. Undefined
   d. Undefined

134. _____ is electromagnetic radiation with a wavelength that is visible to the eye (visible _____) or, in a technical or scientific context, electromagnetic radiation of any wavelength.
   a. Light0
   b. Thing
   c. Undefined
   d. Undefined

135. _____, Greek for "knowledge of nature," is the branch of science concerned with the discovery and characterization of universal laws which govern matter, energy, space, and time.
   a. Physics0
   b. Thing
   c. Undefined
   d. Undefined

136. In mathematics, a matrix can be thought of as each row or _____ being a vector. Hence, a space formed by row vectors or _____ vectors are said to be a row space or a _____ space.
   a. Column0
   b. Concept
   c. Undefined
   d. Undefined

137. _____ is an m × 1 matrix, i.e. a matrix consisting of a single column of m elements.
   a. Column vector0
   b. Thing
   c. Undefined
   d. Undefined

138. In mathematics, a _____ is a rectangular table of numbers or, more generally, a table consisting of abstract quantities that can be added and multiplied.
   a. Thing
   b. Matrix0
   c. Undefined
   d. Undefined

139. _____ means of or relating to the French philosopher and mathematician René Descartes.
   a. Cartesian0
   b. Thing
   c. Undefined
   d. Undefined

140. The _____ is a measurement of how a function changes when the values of its inputs change.
   a. Thing
   b. Derivative0
   c. Undefined
   d. Undefined

Chapter 8. The Integral Theorems of Vector Analysis

141. In mathematics, a _____ is a countable collection of open covers of a topological space that satisfies certain separation axioms.
 a. Thing
 b. Development0
 c. Undefined
 d. Undefined

142. _____ is a binary operation on two vectors in a three-dimensional Euclidean space that results in another vector which is perpedicular to the two input vectors.
 a. Thing
 b. Cross product0
 c. Undefined
 d. Undefined

143. Mathematical _____ is used to represent ideas.
 a. Notation0
 b. Thing
 c. Undefined
 d. Undefined

144. In combinatorial mathematics, a _____ is an un-ordered collection of unique elements.
 a. Combination0
 b. Concept
 c. Undefined
 d. Undefined

145. The word _____ comes from the Latin word linearis, which means created by lines.
 a. Thing
 b. Linear0
 c. Undefined
 d. Undefined

146. In mathematics, the conjugate _____ or adjoint matrix of an m-by-n matrix A with complex entries is the n-by-m matrix A* obtained from A by taking the transpose and then taking the complex conjugate of each entry.
 a. Pairs0
 b. Thing
 c. Undefined
 d. Undefined

147. _____ is bother the congnitive process of transferring information from a particular subject , and a linguistic expression corresponding to such a process.
 a. Thing
 b. Analogy0
 c. Undefined
 d. Undefined

148. In mathematics, a _____ may be described informally as a number that can be given by an infinite decimal representation.
 a. Real number0
 b. Thing
 c. Undefined
 d. Undefined

149. A _____ is a set whose members are members of another set or a set contained within another set.
 a. Thing
 b. Subset0
 c. Undefined
 d. Undefined

150. _____ are groups whose members are members of another set or a set contained within another set.
 a. Subsets0
 b. Thing
 c. Undefined
 d. Undefined

Chapter 8. The Integral Theorems of Vector Analysis

151. In mathematics, _____ is an elementary arithmetic operation. When one of the numbers is a whole number, _____ is the repeated sum of the other number.
   a. Thing
   b. Multiplication0
   c. Undefined
   d. Undefined

152. _____ is a branch of mathematics concerning the study of structure, relation and quantity.
   a. Concept
   b. Algebra0
   c. Undefined
   d. Undefined

153. _____, a field in mathematics, is the study of how functions change when their inputs change. The primary object of study in _____ is the derivative.
   a. Thing
   b. Differential calculus0
   c. Undefined
   d. Undefined

154. _____ of a function of several variables is its derivative with respect to one of those variables with the others held constant as opposed to the total derivative, in which all variables are allowed to vary.
   a. Partial derivative0
   b. Thing
   c. Undefined
   d. Undefined

155. _____ is the study of terms and their use — of words and compound words that are used in specific contexts.
   a. Terminology0
   b. Thing
   c. Undefined
   d. Undefined

156. _____ is a trigonemtric function that is important when studying triangles and modeling periodic phenomena, among other applications.
   a. Sine0
   b. Thing
   c. Undefined
   d. Undefined

157. _____ is the distance around a given two-dimensional object. As a general rule, the _____ of a polygon can always be calculated by adding all the length of the sides together. So, the formula for triangles is P = a + b + c, where a, b and c stand for each side of it. For quadrilaterals the equation is P = a + b + c + d. For equilateral polygons, P = na, where n is the number of sides and a is the side length.
   a. Perimeter0
   b. Thing
   c. Undefined
   d. Undefined

158. A _____ can refer to a line joining two nonadjacent vertices of a polygon or polyhedron, or in some contexts any upward or downward sloping line. .
   a. Thing
   b. Diagonal0
   c. Undefined
   d. Undefined

ANSWER KEY

Chapter 1

1. a	2. b	3. b	4. b	5. b	6. b	7. b	8. a	9. a	10. b
11. b	12. b	13. b	14. a	15. a	16. a	17. a	18. a	19. b	20. a
21. a	22. a	23. a	24. a	25. b	26. b	27. b	28. b	29. b	30. b
31. a	32. a	33. b	34. a	35. b	36. b	37. b	38. b	39. a	40. a
41. a	42. b	43. a	44. b	45. b	46. b	47. b	48. a	49. a	50. b
51. b	52. b	53. a	54. b	55. a	56. b	57. a	58. a	59. b	60. a
61. a	62. a	63. b	64. b	65. b	66. a	67. a	68. a	69. b	70. a
71. a	72. b	73. b	74. a	75. a	76. a	77. a	78. b	79. a	80. a
81. a	82. a	83. a	84. b	85. a	86. a	87. a	88. a	89. b	90. b
91. b	92. b	93. b	94. a	95. b	96. b	97. a	98. b	99. a	100. b
101. a	102. a	103. a	104. a	105. a	106. b	107. a	108. b	109. b	110. a
111. a	112. b	113. a	114. a	115. a	116. a	117. a	118. b	119. b	120. a
121. b	122. b	123. b	124. b	125. b	126. a	127. b	128. b	129. a	130. b
131. a	132. b	133. b	134. b	135. a	136. b	137. a	138. b	139. a	140. a
141. b	142. a	143. a	144. a	145. a	146. a	147. b	148. b	149. b	150. b
151. b	152. b	153. b	154. a	155. b	156. a	157. b	158. b	159. b	160. b
161. a	162. a	163. b	164. b	165. a	166. a	167. a	168. a	169. b	170. b
171. b	172. a	173. b	174. a	175. b	176. a	177. b	178. b	179. b	180. b
181. b	182. a	183. a	184. b	185. b	186. b	187. a	188. b	189. a	190. b
191. a	192. a	193. b	194. b	195. b	196. a	197. a	198. b	199. a	200. b
201. b	202. b	203. b							

Chapter 2

1. a	2. b	3. b	4. b	5. b	6. a	7. b	8. a	9. a	10. a
11. a	12. a	13. b	14. a	15. b	16. b	17. a	18. a	19. b	20. b
21. b	22. b	23. b	24. b	25. a	26. b	27. a	28. a	29. a	30. a
31. b	32. b	33. a	34. b	35. a	36. a	37. b	38. a	39. a	40. a
41. a	42. a	43. b	44. b	45. a	46. b	47. a	48. a	49. a	50. b
51. b	52. a	53. b	54. a	55. a	56. b	57. b	58. b	59. a	60. a
61. b	62. b	63. a	64. b	65. a	66. a	67. a	68. b	69. b	70. b
71. b	72. b	73. a	74. a	75. b	76. b	77. b	78. a	79. b	80. b
81. a	82. a	83. a	84. b	85. b	86. b	87. a	88. b	89. a	90. a
91. a	92. a	93. a	94. b	95. a	96. b	97. a	98. b	99. a	100. b
101. a	102. a	103. a	104. a	105. a	106. b	107. b	108. a	109. a	110. b
111. a	112. a	113. b	114. a	115. a	116. b	117. b	118. a	119. b	120. a
121. b	122. b	123. b	124. a	125. a	126. a	127. b	128. b	129. b	130. b
131. a	132. b	133. b	134. b	135. b	136. a	137. b	138. b	139. b	140. b
141. a	142. a	143. b	144. a	145. a	146. a	147. b	148. a	149. b	150. b
151. b	152. a								

Chapter 3

1. a	2. b	3. b	4. a	5. b	6. b	7. a	8. b	9. a	10. b
11. b	12. b	13. a	14. a	15. b	16. b	17. b	18. a	19. a	20. a
21. a	22. a	23. a	24. a	25. a	26. b	27. b	28. b	29. a	30. a
31. a	32. a	33. b	34. b	35. b	36. b	37. a	38. b	39. b	40. a
41. b	42. a	43. a	44. a	45. b	46. a	47. b	48. a	49. a	50. b
51. b	52. b	53. b	54. a	55. a	56. b	57. b	58. b	59. a	60. a
61. b	62. a	63. a	64. a	65. b	66. a	67. a	68. a	69. a	70. b
71. b	72. a	73. b	74. a	75. b	76. a	77. b	78. a	79. a	80. a
81. a	82. a	83. a	84. b	85. a	86. a	87. b	88. b	89. a	90. b
91. a	92. b	93. b	94. b	95. a	96. a	97. a	98. a	99. a	100. b
101. b	102. b	103. a	104. a	105. a	106. b	107. b	108. b	109. b	110. b
111. a	112. a	113. a	114. a	115. b	116. b	117. a	118. a	119. b	120. a
121. a	122. a	123. a	124. b	125. a	126. b	127. a	128. b	129. b	130. b
131. a	132. a	133. a	134. a	135. b	136. b	137. b	138. b	139. b	140. a
141. b	142. b	143. a	144. b	145. a	146. a	147. a	148. b	149. b	150. b
151. b	152. a	153. a	154. b	155. a	156. a	157. a	158. b	159. b	160. a
161. b	162. a	163. a	164. b	165. a	166. b	167. b	168. a	169. b	170. a
171. a	172. a	173. a	174. a	175. b	176. a	177. a	178. a	179. a	180. a
181. a									

Chapter 4

1. a	2. b	3. b	4. b	5. a	6. b	7. b	8. a	9. b	10. b
11. b	12. b	13. b	14. a	15. b	16. b	17. a	18. b	19. b	20. b
21. b	22. b	23. a	24. b	25. b	26. a	27. b	28. b	29. b	30. b
31. b	32. b	33. a	34. b	35. a	36. b	37. a	38. b	39. a	40. a
41. b	42. a	43. b	44. b	45. a	46. a	47. a	48. b	49. b	50. b
51. a	52. a	53. b	54. b	55. b	56. a	57. b	58. a	59. b	60. b
61. a	62. a	63. a	64. b	65. b	66. b	67. a	68. b	69. a	70. b
71. b	72. a	73. b	74. b	75. a	76. b	77. a	78. b	79. a	80. a
81. a	82. b	83. b	84. a	85. b	86. a	87. b	88. b	89. b	90. b
91. b	92. a	93. b	94. b	95. a	96. a	97. a	98. b	99. b	100. b
101. b	102. a	103. a	104. b	105. b	106. b	107. a	108. b	109. a	110. b
111. b	112. b	113. b	114. b	115. a	116. a	117. b	118. b	119. b	120. b
121. a	122. b	123. b	124. b	125. a	126. b	127. a	128. b	129. b	130. a
131. a	132. b	133. a	134. b	135. b	136. b	137. a	138. a	139. a	140. b
141. a	142. b	143. a	144. a	145. a	146. b	147. a	148. a	149. b	150. a
151. a	152. a	153. b	154. b	155. b	156. b	157. a	158. b	159. b	160. a
161. b	162. a	163. a	164. a	165. a	166. b	167. b	168. a	169. b	170. a
171. b	172. b	173. a							

ANSWER KEY

Chapter 5

1. a	2. a	3. b	4. b	5. a	6. b	7. b	8. a	9. b	10. b
11. b	12. a	13. b	14. b	15. a	16. b	17. b	18. b	19. b	20. b
21. a	22. a	23. a	24. b	25. a	26. b	27. b	28. b	29. b	30. a
31. b	32. b	33. b	34. b	35. b	36. b	37. a	38. a	39. a	40. b
41. b	42. b	43. b	44. b	45. a	46. a	47. b	48. a	49. b	50. a
51. a	52. b	53. a	54. a	55. a	56. a	57. a	58. b	59. a	60. a
61. a	62. a	63. b	64. a	65. b	66. a	67. b	68. b	69. a	70. a
71. b	72. a	73. b	74. a	75. a	76. b	77. a	78. a	79. a	80. b
81. b	82. a	83. b	84. b	85. a	86. b	87. a	88. b	89. b	90. b
91. b									

Chapter 6

1. b	2. b	3. b	4. b	5. a	6. a	7. a	8. b	9. b	10. b
11. b	12. a	13. a	14. b	15. a	16. a	17. b	18. b	19. b	20. a
21. a	22. b	23. b	24. b	25. b	26. a	27. a	28. a	29. b	30. b
31. b	32. b	33. a	34. a	35. a	36. a	37. a	38. b	39. b	40. a
41. a	42. a	43. a	44. b	45. b	46. b	47. a	48. b	49. a	50. a
51. b	52. a	53. b	54. b	55. b	56. a	57. b	58. b	59. a	60. a
61. b	62. b	63. a	64. b	65. a	66. b	67. a	68. b	69. a	70. a
71. b	72. b	73. b	74. b	75. b	76. a	77. a	78. b	79. a	80. b
81. b	82. a	83. b	84. a	85. a	86. b	87. b	88. a	89. b	90. a
91. a	92. b	93. b	94. b	95. a	96. b	97. a	98. a	99. a	100. a
101. b	102. a	103. b	104. a	105. b	106. b	107. a	108. a	109. a	110. b
111. b	112. b	113. b	114. b	115. b	116. b	117. b	118. a	119. a	120. a
121. b	122. b	123. b	124. b	125. b	126. b	127. a			

Chapter 7

1. a	2. b	3. a	4. a	5. b	6. a	7. b	8. b	9. b	10. b
11. b	12. a	13. a	14. b	15. b	16. b	17. a	18. a	19. a	20. a
21. a	22. b	23. b	24. a	25. b	26. a	27. b	28. b	29. b	30. b
31. b	32. b	33. b	34. b	35. b	36. b	37. a	38. b	39. b	40. a
41. b	42. b	43. b	44. b	45. b	46. a	47. a	48. b	49. a	50. b
51. a	52. b	53. b	54. b	55. b	56. a	57. a	58. a	59. a	60. b
61. b	62. a	63. a	64. a	65. b	66. a	67. a	68. a	69. b	70. a
71. a	72. b	73. b	74. a	75. a	76. a	77. a	78. b	79. a	80. b
81. a	82. a	83. b	84. b	85. b	86. b	87. a	88. b	89. a	90. b
91. b	92. a	93. a	94. b	95. a	96. a	97. b	98. a	99. a	100. b
101. a	102. b	103. b	104. a	105. a	106. a	107. a	108. b	109. b	110. b
111. b	112. a	113. b	114. b	115. b	116. a	117. a	118. a	119. a	120. a
121. a	122. a	123. b	124. a	125. b	126. a	127. b	128. b	129. b	130. b
131. a	132. b	133. b	134. a	135. b	136. b	137. b	138. a	139. a	140. a
141. a	142. a	143. a	144. a	145. a	146. a	147. b	148. b	149. b	150. b
151. b	152. b	153. b	154. b	155. b	156. a	157. a	158. b	159. b	160. a
161. b	162. a	163. b	164. b	165. b	166. a	167. b	168. a	169. b	170. a
171. b	172. b	173. a	174. b	175. b	176. a	177. b	178. a	179. b	180. b
181. b	182. a	183. b							

Chapter 8

1. a	2. a	3. b	4. b	5. a	6. a	7. b	8. a	9. b	10. b
11. a	12. b	13. b	14. b	15. b	16. a	17. a	18. b	19. b	20. a
21. a	22. b	23. b	24. b	25. b	26. a	27. b	28. a	29. b	30. b
31. a	32. b	33. b	34. b	35. a	36. a	37. a	38. a	39. b	40. b
41. b	42. b	43. a	44. a	45. a	46. a	47. a	48. b	49. a	50. b
51. b	52. a	53. b	54. a	55. b	56. a	57. a	58. b	59. a	60. a
61. a	62. a	63. a	64. b	65. a	66. a	67. a	68. a	69. a	70. a
71. a	72. a	73. b	74. a	75. b	76. a	77. a	78. a	79. b	80. b
81. b	82. a	83. b	84. a	85. b	86. a	87. b	88. a	89. a	90. b
91. a	92. a	93. a	94. a	95. b	96. a	97. a	98. a	99. b	100. a
101. a	102. b	103. b	104. b	105. a	106. a	107. a	108. b	109. a	110. b
111. b	112. b	113. a	114. b	115. a	116. a	117. b	118. a	119. a	120. b
121. a	122. b	123. a	124. a	125. a	126. b	127. a	128. b	129. a	130. a
131. b	132. a	133. a	134. a	135. a	136. a	137. a	138. b	139. a	140. a
141. b	142. a	143. a	144. a	145. b	146. a	147. b	148. a	149. b	150. a
151. b	152. b	153. b	154. a	155. a	156. a	157. a	158. b		